2—

IT'S ONLY

A GAME

IT'S ONLY A GAME

WORDS OF WISDOM FROM A LIFETIME IN GOLF

JACKIE BURKE, JR.

WITH

GUY YOCOM

GOTHAM BOOKS

GOTHAM BOOKS
Published by Penguin Group (USA) Inc.
375 Hudson Street, New York, New York 10014, U.S.A.

Penguin Group (Canada), 90 Eglinton Avenue East, Suite 700, Toronto, Ontario M4P 2Y3, Canada (a division of Pearson Penguin Canada Inc.); Penguin Books Ltd, 80 Strand, London WC2R 0RL, England; Penguin Ireland, 25 St Stephen's Green, Dublin 2, Ireland (a division of Penguin Books Ltd); Penguin Group (Australia), 250 Camberwell Road, Camberwell, Victoria 3124, Australia (a division of Pearson Australia Group Pty Ltd); Penguin Books India Pvt Ltd, 11 Community Centre, Panchsheel Park, New Delhi - 110 017, India; Penguin Group (NZ), cnr Airborne and Rosedale Roads, Albany, Auckland 1310, New Zealand (a division of Pearson New Zealand Ltd); Penguin Books (South Africa) (Pty) Ltd, 24 Sturdee Avenue, Rosebank, Johannesburg 2196, South Africa

Penguin Books Ltd, Registered Offices: 80 Strand, London WC2R 0RL, England

Published by Gotham Books, a division of Penguin Group (USA) Inc.

First printing, March 2006
10   9   8   7   6   5   4

Gotham Books and the skyscraper logo are trademarks of Penguin Group (USA) Inc.

LIBRARY OF CONGRESS CATALOGING-IN-PUBLICATION DATA
has been applied for.

ISBN 1-592-40116-3

Printed in the United States of America
Set in Bodoni
Designed by Ginger Legato

To all the amateurs across the world:
The only difference between a good player and a poor player
is that the good player didn't quit.
I hope you enjoy this little book. It's for you.
Take a deep breath—it's only a game!

JACKIE BURKE, JR.,

HOUSTON, TEXAS

DECEMBER 2005

CONTENTS

by

BEN CRENSHAW

When I was fifteen, my father invited me to drive with him to Houston, where he was playing in the Champions Cup Invitational. My game was beginning to blossom, and Dad was hoping that Jackie Burke might find time to take a look at my swing. Harvey Penick was always my main teacher, but a lot of what Harvey knew came from Jackie's father, Jack Burke, Sr. Thus, Dad felt that some input from Jackie would do my game a world of good.

The first thing I noticed about Jackie—and the feature that gets my attention still—was his eyes. The Burkes all were blessed with ice-blue eyes. He looked at me and it was like he was searching my soul. He took the measure of me, and over the next couple of days communicated not so much verbally as with a stare, a glare, and sometimes a twinkle. Jackie's eyes could show kindness, sympathy, understanding, and humor. Other times those eyes were more ice than blue, his disdain or disgust impossible to conceal.

I got an awful lot out of those first lessons, for my putting especially. Jackie told me not to putt on such a precise line to the hole, to stop being so exacting. "When you putt," he said, "imagine a wide line of Sherwin-Williams paint going from your ball to the hole. Get your ball rolling on that big, fat line as best you can. You're not good enough to be trying to putt on a skinny little line, because you're human. If you get too precise, you'll freeze up. Widen your line; give yourself some latitude. You need it." That was one of the best putting lessons I ever received.

Many years after that meeting, I came back to Champions Golf Club to watch the Nabisco Championships, a precursor to the Tour Championship. I didn't qualify for the tournament and was terribly disappointed. Jack noticed I was feeling down and invited me to walk in the gallery with him. On the third hole he said, "Ben, what do you notice about this tournament that is different from every other tournament on the PGA Tour?" I looked around and didn't see anything special.

"I don't know, Jackie," I said.

He said, "Can't you see there is not one golf cart out here? Not even for the tour staff, the TV people, nobody? What do you think is the reason for that?"

"I don't know, Jackie," I said.

Jackie stopped and patted the right pocket of his pants. "Because the keys to every cart on the property are right here in this pocket, and nobody knows where they are except me." His eyes had that twinkle.

I couldn't stop laughing. Jackie loathes golf carts, and the thought of all the important people trying in vain to get a golf cart cracked me up. Jackie is a kid at heart, and the impishness of that pointed practical joke brightened my day.

I've gone periods without seeing Jackie and have yearned for his company. Being with him is like a tonic for the soul. But a trip to Champions is never what I expect. I always anticipate a breezy conversation, a golf lesson filled with import and wisdom, a relaxing meal in which we discuss everything under the sun—Jackie is current and very well read, you know.

But he always surprises me. Golf is supposed to be a serene game, but a lesson from Jackie Burke is a full-contact sport. He'll whack you just before you take the club back and tell you you're off balance. Or because he's taken tae kwon do, he'll remind you he can take your knee out with one kick. I've been tempted to show up for a lesson wearing a face mask, chest protector, and shin guards. He wants you to leave Champions with more than a warm and fuzzy feeling. He wants you to leave having learned something about the game, so you can play better and enjoy it more.

Jackie is a warrior. He is a born competitor who meets every challenge head on, on and off the golf course. Whether it's about getting a good deal on a fleet of the golf carts he hates, negotiating a TV contract, trying to help the amateurs at Champions play better, or trying to beat you out of a five-dollar nassau, he is constantly competing to make himself and the people and world around him better. He is fiercely protective of the game, his club, his family and friends. His values and integrity are unassailable, as pure as those of any man I've known.

These days, those ice-blue eyes of Jackie's mostly reveal vitality, joy, enthusiasm, curiosity, and a deep inner happiness toward life and where it's taken him. He is full to the brim with living each day to its fullest. He is always looking forward, never back. I always leave Champions with more knowledge about the game, a deeper appreciation for the talent I was given, and thankfulness that I chose golf as my profession. Mostly I feel a deep sense of gratitude for having this extraordinary man in my life. Jackie Burke is the rare and great man every person should be privileged to know.

by

STEVE ELKINGTON

The smartest decision I made as a young pro was buying a house next door to Jackie Burke. On the mornings when I wasn't on the road playing the PGA Tour, I'd stop by Jackie's house for breakfast and conversation. We'd been friends since my college days at the University of Houston, but when we became neighbors we grew even closer. Our morning huddles became such a habit that we named our association "The Breakfast Club" and had T-shirts made up with our club's name on the front. It was during these informal breakfasts that my advanced education in golf and life began.

On the wall of Jackie and Robin's kitchen is a plaque containing the Ten Commands. Not commandments, mind you, but *commands*. It's a list of original adages, dictums, and directives that Jackie has hammered home to his kids and close friends over the years, and which they one day decided to compile. If you want to know what Jackie Burke is about, you can find out just by reading the list. They apply to both golf and life, and he touches on a few of them in this book.

I can recite the Ten Commands from memory. They are:

1. **First things first.** Jackie talks a lot about the importance of prioritizing, of never getting ahead of yourself. When I was young and asked Jackie what it was like playing in a major championship, he told me to remember this rule, because when I stepped onto the first tee my first task was to get a tee out of my pocket, and that it might not be easy because I'd be so nervous. He told me to think of the shot I'm playing, not the ones coming up. It applies to life, too. So many mistakes are made because you get ahead of yourself in your thinking.

2. **The 50-51 Rule.** Jackie got this from a Catholic priest when he was a boy. It basically means that if you have $50, don't spend $51. The temptation to live beyond your means is considerable, even for people with good incomes. You can be thrifty without being frugal.

3. **My way or the highway.** This isn't quite as harsh as it sounds. In any organization, one person ultimately must be in charge. That person should seek advice, delegate responsibility, and accept criticism, but at the end of the day his word is law. Only one person should be in command.

4. **Anything with its head down gets eaten.** As you'll discover in this book, Jackie believes golf and life are analogous to the animal kingdom and primitive man. When Jackie utters this particular command, he speaks of the importance of being alert and observant. In golf, it liter-

ally means keeping your head up as you walk so you can note which way the wind is blowing or which way another player's ball breaks on the green. In life, it means staying current with news and social trends.

5. **Be like the leopard on the limb.** The leopard doesn't pounce from the tree for the first animal that passes beneath. He's patient and waits for something particularly healthy and tasty. The golfer, meanwhile, shouldn't go for every par 5 in two or attack every pin. Nor should the consumer buy the first TV he sees in the store window or buy every stock he reads about. You need to show patience and restraint.

6. **If you can put a match to it, it's not worth anything.** Jackie is what I call a relationship guy. He values people much more than material things. He doesn't drive an expensive car, live in a huge house, or live extravagantly in any way. He believes happiness can only be attained by cultivating good friendships and a happy family environment.

7. **Apples don't fall far from the tree.** Children inherit the physical traits of their parents and some of their emotional ones. The smart parent knows that some of a child's tendencies are simply passed down by them, and they work with them and around them. But for the most part, the quality of a child's character is acquired through the examples set by his or her parents.

xvi · STEVE ELKINGTON

8. **Your clubs don't know if it's raining.** Don't blame outside influences for your failure, or give them too much credit when you succeed. Make a point of being 100-percent accountable for your actions, even when circumstances contribute to a less than desirable result.

9. **You can't take it with you.** Jackie likes to point out that you never see a Brinks truck in a funeral procession. Be philanthropic. Enjoy life. Leave something behind for your spouse and children, but not so much that they never learn the importance of hard work or making their own way in the world.

10. **The two key words to a successful marriage are "Yes, Dear."** This rule is not sexist, because it applies to both parties. Men and women both need a sympathetic ear on occasion.

It's no secret that Jackie has been my golf teacher. He prepared me for a career on the PGA Tour by refining my golf swing, sharpening my short game and improving my putting. He helped me become a better competitor and smarter course manager. A great deal of his teaching philosophy is in this book, and it's wonderful to read and apply to your game.

But today Jackie is much more than that. Through the Ten Commands and a hundred other chunks of wisdom, and his loyal friendship, he became my spiritual advisor, sports psychologist, sounding board, cheerleader, surrogate parent, confidante. Without knowing it, he did a great deal to make me a better, more well-rounded person.

This book is pure Jackie, and I hope that from reading it you get some of the fulfillment and enjoyment he's given to me and others over the years.

by

TIM FINCHEM

Jackie Burke is as passionate about the game of golf as anyone I have ever met. His passion often results in some interesting and sometimes humorous commentary.

The first time I met Jackie, we were seated next to each other at a dinner at a Shell Houston Open. After a few minutes of pleasantries, Jackie inquired as to whether I was familiar with the people at the United States Golf Association. I responded that I thought we had a good working relationship with the staff and members of the executive committee. Jackie asked me if I would do him a favor and explain to those folks that the initials "USGA" stood for *United States* Golf Association, not the New York/New Jersey Golf Association. That was the beginning of learning what Jackie Burke is all about.

Several years later, we had entered into an agreement to play the Tour Championship at Jackie's Champions Golf Club. On arrival at the tournament he asked to sit down with me. He was concerned about two things: one, that in writing up the site agreement to play the tournament at Champions we had used the term *venue*. Jackie wanted me to know in no uncertain terms that when he was playing on the PGA Tour, he played on golf courses, not venues. The other thing he was concerned about was the fact that his tee markers had been replaced with ones that indicated the name of the title sponsor, an automobile manufacturer. He thought this was extreme commercialism and detrimental to the presentation of the game. Years later, on his eightieth birthday, we gave Jackie a miniaturized teeing ground with synthetic grass adorned with two of these tee markers. Such is the relationship that has developed over the years.

I love and respect many things about Jackie Burke, including his history as a player, his integrity, his teaching capability, and his incredible sense of humor. The one thing that impresses me more than any other, however, is the product of his work to build a golf club.

Champions in every respect is a manifestation of Jackie's passion for the game and competition. The nature of the members, the number of outstanding tournaments it has hosted, and the total focus on understanding golf as an unparalleled game comes through at Champions.

I've always enjoyed the occasions we've conducted the Tour Championship at Champions. The Cypress Creek Course there is one of the sternest tests of golf in America and for forty years has held its own against the best players in the world. Champions also exudes a "golfy" atmosphere that is rare, and difficult for other courses to duplicate. This is reflected in the opinions of our players, who enjoy competing where golf is understood and appreciated.

Jackie embodies all that is great about the game and the people who play it. He is always a source of wisdom and advice. His knowledge is so vast, his range of experiences so diverse, and his insight into golf and life so spot-on, that I always come away richer for the experience. I've never known anyone like him.

The qualities about Jackie that I enjoy so much personally come across clearly in this book. Sit back and enjoy—you're in for a real treat.

by

JIM MCLEAN

In the summer of 1971, I finished among the top eight in the U.S. Amateur, which earned me an invitation to play in the Masters the following spring. I was attending the University of Houston at the time and had gotten to know Jackie Burke. I sought Jackie's counsel often while I was in school and, with the Masters some months away, asked him one day for some advice on driving the ball under pressure.

"I suggest you drive to Galveston and drive a couple of balls into the Gulf of Mexico," Jackie said. "That will teach you all you really need to know."

That seemed to me like some odd advice. To be truthful I sort of dismissed it. But one day, some friends and I drove to Galveston to spend some time at the beach. When we pulled in, Jackie's suggestion suddenly came to mind. I got my driver out of the trunk of my car, walked down to the beach, teed three balls in the firm sand overlooking the Gulf of Mexico, and drove the balls into the water. If there was a revelation in that, I didn't know what it was.

Some time later, when I visited Jackie out at Champions, I mentioned that I'd done what he'd said.

"Well, what did you learn from it?" he asked.

"I'm not sure," I said.

"How well did you hit those balls?" he persisted.

"Pretty good," I said. "The Gulf of Mexico is a pretty big target."

"That's it!" Jackie exclaimed. "When you play, you've got to see the fairway as though it's the Gulf of Mexico—too big to miss. If you try to steer the ball out there with the driver, you're dead."

I received two good lessons from that experience—one about driving and the other about Jackie. When you talk golf with Jackie, his very meaningful points sometimes go missing because he is so demonstrative, so intense and downright entertaining. That's why I write down what he tells me—and why he refers to me in this book as "the note-takingest son of a gun I've ever seen."

In this book, Jackie conveys some terrific instruction for players of all levels. Jackie is, above all else, a teacher. He doesn't merely help players; he helps fellows like me teach the game better. Virtually all of the success I've had in the teaching profession can be attributed to the principles he conveyed to me over the years. In looking over my notes, I found a few of his thoughts for teachers. I'd like to share these with my colleagues.

- **Learn to size up your students.** Take note of every move they make, what they say, and how they say it. Note their facial expressions. Their swings are a reflection of their personalities, so learn their personalities!

- **Make every student better, in some way, with every lesson.** Improving the full swing is a gradual progress, but you must make the progress noticeable. The student must feel he is getting something for his time and money, and you must provide a return on his investment.

- **Learn everything about golf.** Become a towering expert on all phases of the game, not just the swing. Know its history, the rules, the players, etiquette, equipment, and even a little about agronomy. The word *professional* implies you are an authority. Try to live up to that.

- **Demonstrate passion and enthusiasm.** If you genuinely love teaching and let it show, your student can't help but be a better learner. It should be an exercise in fun, a stimulating experience for both of you.

- **Listen to the pupils.** Don't gloss over their reactions to what you've asked them to do. They're giving you insight into the quality of your advice.

- **Be a fanatic on details.** Be able to describe the same movement three different ways. Break it down until your objective hits home. Increase your vocabulary.

This sampling of advice to teachers is a further example of Jackie's wisdom. There is one more personal anecdote I'd like to relate. Many years ago, when I left Texas in search of a club professional job in the New York area, I confronted an obstacle that is peculiar to the club-pro industry. That is, clubs traditionally like to hire men who are married, perhaps because it is a sign of personal stability. I wasn't married yet and was very concerned as to how I would overcome my bachelor status in the job interviews. I phoned xxvi · JIM McLEAN

Jackie, and he promptly cited twenty reasons why my being single would be an asset instead of a liability.

Over the next several years I interviewed at several outstanding clubs: Westchester, Tamarisk, Sunningdale, Quaker Ridge, and Sleepy Hollow. I got every job.

Jackie Burke is the most interesting person I've ever met. His influence has extended across the entire landscape of golf. Even those who don't know him personally are beneficiaries of his desire to make the game better for all of us. I'm very proud to call him my good friend.

by

PHIL MICKELSON

Jackie Burke is old-school, in a good way. He doesn't want to go back to wooden shafts and lumpy golf balls. But he doesn't want to spend hours videotaping your swing and overanalyzing it to death, either. He just loves the game and loves seeing players improve their games the old-fashioned way, through hard work and determination.

Golf can be a hard game. Jackie likes to say there are no quick fixes, and it will take time to do what he says. Not to understand it, but to execute it. When I first went to see him in 1999, he introduced me to the three-foot putting drill—make a hundred in a row from a three-foot circle around the hole. Jackie explains the details of that lesson in this book, and I hope I'm not giving too much away when I say that after I got home, it took me three days before I could hole a hundred three-footers consecutively. Now, years later, it takes me about twenty minutes. I do it in preparation for all my tournaments. In the past I was sort of known for missing short putts, but after listening to Jackie and spending time, lots of time, I can't remember missing a putt inside three feet and that's helped me win the 2004 Masters and 2005 PGA Championship. That's the hard-work part.

As for determination, you'd better have as much as Jackie does if you want to improve under his watch. Billy Ray Brown, who has shared this story with me and probably a lot of others, was an All-American at Houston before he joined the tour and went on to a career in television. He once called Jackie to get some help with his putting. Jackie was impressed that Billy Ray, knowing he was a good player, felt he wanted to get even better with some help. So Jackie invited Billy Ray to Champions for lessons.

The first putt was a routine six-footer. Billy Ray missed and, easygoing guy that he is, didn't react with enough anguish to suit Jackie. Out of nowhere Jackie smacked Billy Ray upside the head. Stunned, Billy Ray looked up to see Jackie's scowling face.

"Son, I want you to feel *pain* when you miss a putt," roared Jackie.

It's pretty simple with Jackie Burke. When you work with him you have to care, really care, about getting better, because he does. And you have to take the time to work at it, because it'll take time. He's a great man who has helped me and thousands of other golfers. I've never met anyone who loves the game more or has such desire to make it more enjoyable for others.

I look forward to getting back to Champions to see him again. I want to make a hundred in a row and win back the dinner I lost. But I'm going to insist on one rule: If I miss, there's no hitting. You listening, Jackie?

by

HAL SUTTON

The year before I turned pro, I came to Houston to play in the annual Champions Cup Invitational. It's one of the best amateur tournaments in the nation, a two-man team event that draws many of the best players in the country. My partner and I played very well and won the tournament, which, along with my winning the U.S. Amateur that summer, helped confirm that my decision to turn pro in the near future was a sound one.

After the awards ceremony, I asked Jackie if he would meet with me briefly and give me a bit of advice on what to expect when I got out on the PGA Tour. He agreed and led me to a porch outside the Champions clubhouse. The porch is elevated a few feet above the ground, and without my knowing it, Jackie positioned me on the porch's precipice.

"So, Mr. Burke, what's my first year as a pro out there going to be like?" I asked.

Jackie paused, then suddenly gave me a quick push. Taken totally by surprise, I flailed my arms as I tried to avoid falling off the porch. Fortunately, I recovered my balance just in time. I looked at him with what I'm sure was an expression of total shock.

"*That's* what the tour is going to be like," he said. "That moment where you felt yourself going off the edge, that surge of butterflies in your stomach, that feeling of being totally off balance—that's more or less how you're going to feel every day when you get out there."

After I digested what Jackie had said—and moved away from the edge of the porch—I asked him to go into more detail.

"Nobody is going to be awed by you, Hal," he said. "You can't expect the other players to help you. This is the real deal, son. It's going to be a game of survival out there. The other guys are not your friends, at least not at first. They are not going to be happy having another young player out there trying to take a cut out of their living.

"You're going to see some things you aren't used to," he continued. "You're going to have a guy slow-play you. You might see a guy take a drop you don't think is right, and you're going to be faced with the prospect of either giving in to that or refusing to sign his scorecard.

"What I'm saying is, you better toughen up, earn some respect, and learn to stay balanced when somebody gives you a push, because you are going to be pushed every single day."

It was the best lesson about the tour I could have asked for. Jackie has been one of my closest friends and confidantes ever since. Whenever I needed advice, support, and total honesty, I could always phone Jackie or make a special trip to Houston to see him. I owe him a great deal.

When I was named captain of the 2004 Ryder Cup team, one of the first things I did was select Jackie as a co-captain (Steve Jones was the other). As I saw it, I was doing my team—and myself—a big favor simply by having him in our company. The young players especially stood to benefit from his wisdom, experience, and directness. They also would enjoy his sense of humor and storytelling. He's one of the great characters in golf.

Neither my captaining, Jackie's presence, nor the effort from our players was enough to stave off a bitter defeat to the Europeans, which rates as one of the great disappointments of my career. But as time passes, I appreciate even more what an honor it was to be a Ryder Cup captain, and I reflect back on the experience with more happiness than sadness. As he had been at a lot of important moments in my life, Jackie Burke was right there with me.

I still need Jackie. Last year I began working seriously on a very ambitious golf course design project near Fredericksburg, Texas, close to where Jackie has a second home. I hounded him for advice on many aspects of the project, and as always he came through.

People come and go in your life, but Jackie has been a constant. A man never had a better friend.

IT'S ONLY
A GAME

CHAPTER ONE

THE ONE-EYED DOGS ARE LOOSE

GURUS, HOT DRIVERS, AND WALL-TO-WALL GREEN

If I've learned one thing in my eighty-two years, it's that man has a deep inner desire to dominate. We're consumed with making everything around us bend to our will. It's how we've climbed the tallest mountains, circumnavigated the globe, made great strides in conquering disease, famine, poverty, you name it. Heck, we couldn't look at the moon without wanting to gain dominion over it somehow, and eventually we planted a flag there, too. (I tip my hat to the three astronauts who have been members at Champions: Charles Duke, Alan Shepard, and Gene Cernan.)

Golf is a ripe target for the domination impulse. Teachers and equipment manufacturers recognize this part of human nature and try their best to exploit it. Instructors throw around words like "system" and "secret" with the tacit suggestion (and a $300-per-hour price tag) that there is an end-all method to perfecting the golf swing. Equipment manufacturers pour millions of dollars and all their technological know-how into inventing clubs and balls that make our shots fly straight and insanely far. Country clubs try to dominate each other by having the best-conditioned course and poshest clubhouse.

It's pervasive. The entities I mention are like one-eyed dogs in a meat shop, blind to everything but the opportunity in front of them and hungry to devour all they can. They feed off the illusion that every facet of the game can be mastered by money, technology, or mechanical know-how. But it's a vicious circle. The equipment makes the golf courses play too short, so golf course builders produce back-breaking golf courses that cost a fortune to create and maintain.

And golf costs more across the board, from drivers that cost $700 to lessons costing $300 an hour to balls that set you back $50 for a dozen. Green fees are off the charts and joining a private club costs more than a college education. It's no wonder the game isn't growing.

Games aren't meant to be dominated. They are intended to be an endless exploration of your skill and intellect, your competitiveness, your physical prowess and desire. They should be impossible to master completely; that adds to the enjoyment. Consider the reason you stopped playing tic-tac-toe at age ten: You solved the challenge, and thus it ceased being remotely interesting. Golf can never be conquered. The idea of making eighteen consecutive holes in one is crazy, but if it ever happened, someone would tell the player, "Bet you can't do it again next week."

The upward escalation of the game I love has been conducted under the guise of making it better and more fun. But not so ironically, the game is getting harder, not easier, at least for the everyday player. The average handicap of amateurs nationally has been stuck at eighteen for the last forty years. Not everyone has found it worth the cost; we hear about the new people who are constantly streaming into golf, but what about the ones who leave? The numbers aren't really growing. It's plain that the game hasn't become any easier or more fun. It just costs more.

A man, a plan, a canal . . .

Historians tell us the French were the first to take a run at building the Panama Canal. They had a regimented plan for making the monumental construction project work, but when the plan hit some snags, the French withdrew. They didn't have the flexibility to pull it off.

Enter the Americans. We took over the canal and never stopped digging. We dealt with problems as they arose. Like jazz musicians, we never knew where the song was going next. When our engineers encountered a problem, they solved it with old-fashioned American ingenuity. We finished the canal. To this day it's one of the wonders of the world.

Where does golf come to play in this tale? There shouldn't be a "way." We don't need or want teaching systems, which fail miserably anyway—I've never seen one that worked. We don't want or need to bring the game to its knees with equipment that goes against the spirit of the rules (if not the letter of the law). We don't need to kill every last weed on every golf course.

Let's stop looking for ways to circumvent the fundamental challenge of the game, and tackle the game the old-fashioned way—by working on our golf swings. Like the builders of the Panama Canal, we'll deal with legitimate problems as they arise. If that means creating better strains of grass that withstand heat and require less water, fine. If it means building a golf ball that doesn't cut as easily, great. Those are real solutions to real problems. But not being able to drive the ball 270 yards is not a "problem" that needs millions of dollars and changes in the rule book.

We should keep our heads down and enjoy the game for what it is.

Fat chance

If you want a set of irons similar to the ones used by players on the PGA Tour, it will cost you about $750. That's a powerful sum of money, too much for most people. One way to solve that would be for manufacturers to lower their profit margins. But that's like asking a fox not to eat the chickens.

Another solution is to find a set of irons you like and play them for years. Iron club designs have gotten to a point where they can't get much better, so you can buy a set without fearing they'll be obsolete tomorrow. And there's a lot to be said for playing the same set year after year. You really get to know the nuances of the clubs and you build your swing around them.

I admit, though, that trying out and buying new clubs is part of the fun of the game. For the adult who really loves golf, I put that thrill right up there next to buying a new car. I don't know of a purchase that is so capable of making an adult react like a kid at Christmas. But be careful. I've seen careers damaged by players switching to a new line of clubs. Payne Stewart, Johnny Miller, Corey Pavin, and Lee Janzen are some recent examples. Conversely, I've never seen a career take off just because the player put new irons in his bag.

The bottom line

Equipment is a performance factor in every sport. The bat in baseball, the bow in archery, the racquet in tennis, and the driver in golf

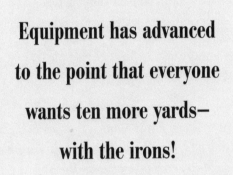

**Equipment has advanced
to the point that everyone
wants ten more yards—
with the irons!**

all make a difference. The question is, how much? I'd say 15 percent is generous. Always remember that poor technique, lousy concentration, and a hundred other human frailties can render the equipment valueless.

Easy money

When a 15-handicapper tells me he likes a certain ball because it spins better around the greens, I just smile and suggest he go buy a few dozen. Why ruin his fun? But I'd bet that if you blacked out the names on ten balls, put them near the practice green, and had the fifteen-handicapper hit some chips and pitches, he couldn't name his ball of choice 10 percent of the time. The same goes for the range. Let him hit as many drivers with the ten balls as he likes. He won't be able to tell the difference.

The up side of modern equipment

It's truly amazing how, over the last fifteen years, a simple stick has become as complex and up-to-date as the space shuttle. It has taken golf talk to a whole new level. You hear stuff like, "I tried the new bi-matrix shaft with the low kick point and liked it, but the launch monitor says a high kick point is better for me. I don't know what to do." I enjoy listening to players rattle on about their club specs. I don't understand half of what they're saying, but I enjoy it. They really love the game.

Watch out for trends

In the 1980s, there was a trend toward "feather-light" irons. There was a notion that standard clubs were too heavy, and that if they were lighter across the board, players could swing them faster and hit the ball farther.

The trend lasted less than a year. Players discovered that they couldn't play golf without feel, and where there's no weight there's no feel. Be wary of breakthrough trends in equipment. There are plenty of challenges to overcome in golf, and our equipment shouldn't be one of them.

How the Burkes missed the boat

My father was a very creative man. He was out driving his car one day in the 1930s when a tire blew out. Eventually a man showed up with a spare and changed the tire. As my dad watched, he noticed that the blown-out tire had nylon cord running through it. Suddenly he had an epiphany. He figured a similar design might be useful on the rubber grips that had just been introduced in golf. One of the problems with the early grips was that they deteriorated quickly and became hard and slippery. Players had an awful time trying to keep a firm hold, especially when it rained. Sometimes clubs would fly from players' hands.

Dad figured that meshing the nylon cord in with the rubber would help the golfer get a better purchase with his hands. And he put the idea into action. A patent was established and the first cord grips made their appearance. Golfers loved them.

While I was in the Marines during World War II, Dad had a sudden heart attack and died. When the war ended and I returned home, I investigated the status of the cord grips, from which our family stood to make a steady profit in the years ahead. I found that the patent had expired and another company had picked it up. So much for that idea.

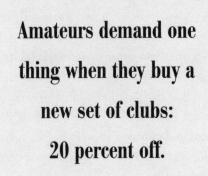

Amateurs demand one thing when they buy a new set of clubs: 20 percent off.

The cord grip is popular to this day. Millions of them have been produced in the years since Dad invented the first one. Imagine having a nickel for every one of them.

Easy come, easy go.

Death of the long irons

Golf club manufacturers owe a dime on every dollar to the modern course architects. They are the reason Vijay Singh carries a 9-wood and people are buying these hybrid clubs that are a cross between a wood and an iron. Firm greens and fairways mean you need a club to get the ball in the air. Why the manufacturers continue to include 2- and 3-irons in their standard sets is beyond me, because the average golfer doesn't have a prayer with these clubs. As for the 1-iron . . . please.

LEAVE WELL ENOUGH ALONE

In praise of "bad" courses

Golf courses in the early part of the twentieth century were often designed and built by amateurs as a one-time thing. In most cases the amateur owned the course he designed, so he poured his heart and soul into it. These courses rarely were very good, even by standards of the time. Mistakes were part of their charm—poor drainage somewhere, a quirky hole or two with misplaced bunkers and misshaped greens, inconsistent turf, et cetera. A course was just as likely to have seven or eleven holes as eighteen, depending on how much property the owner had to work with.

The courses were accepted for what they were. Sometimes they managed to improve over time, as the amateur gradually learned about agronomy and greenkeeping. Even when he didn't, the owner generally took pride in his creation and had a vested interest in its success. It was the only course he had ever designed or ever would, and consequently he was devoted to it.

These mom-and-pop operations were distinctive and had a pleasant atmosphere. They were affordable and gave working-class people and kids a place to play. I always thought they were a nice counterpoint to the posh clubs near the metropolitan areas, sort of like a sandlot baseball field compared to a major league stadium. Sadly, most of them no longer exist. They were simply torn up and sold for real estate developments, or went to seed because the owners lost money trying to operate them. Municipal and daily-fee courses are common today, of course, but aren't quite the same thing. Even the most accessible ones are at least slightly overpriced because cities want them to be profit centers. Some have a homey atmosphere, but many do not.

I think our standards for golf courses today are too high. We seem obsessed with our courses being a fine line of perfect from start to finish. Anything less than the Gardens of Babylon is deemed unacceptable. Golf course superintendents are under tremendous pressure these days. Job security is a big issue. Greenkeepers are as stressed as air traffic controllers. Like any consumers, golfers want their money's worth, and if there's a brown spot near the fourteenth fairway, they want someone's head to roll.

It's gotten out of hand. It saddens me to hear an 18-handicapper refer to a course as a "dog track" or a "dump." Those terms are a reflection of that person's perspective and values, which have become warped. They see the Masters on television and think, "Why can't my course look like that?" Well, it can, provided you've got a maintenance budget in the millions of dollars. Most golfers don't understand that and don't want to. They just want that wall-to-wall green—unless they're watching the British Open. Then the color brown becomes charming. It's insane.

Golf courses should be accepted on their own terms. The U.S. Open has only been held in Texas once in the last sixty-five years (Champions hosted it in 1969), and Florida has *never* hosted a U.S. Open, which is just unbelievable considering the number of courses and the way golfers there are crazy about the game. The USGA just won't do it, in part because it's difficult getting the greens the way they like them—lightning-fast and firm.

Keep in mind, I have no quarrel with modern golf course architects. They do a fabulous job, especially on their biggest, grandest projects. The cute cosmetic touches, the jigsaw-puzzle bunkers, the same firmness of turf from start to finish, it's all great. I'm just alarmed by the standard they've set for everyone else.

Some bargain
These high-end public courses can't possibly work. A family of four for $400? When it's over you look in your wallet and think, "I hope the kids don't ask if we can do this again tomorrow."

Flights of fancy
Golf is really in your blood when you drive through a strange area and start envisioning golf courses on every pretty piece of property around the next bend. This is what happened with Jimmy Demaret and me when we envisioned Champions. We looked at several pieces of property, but the land here looked just right for a golf course.

Real golfers can't keep those thoughts out. These are waking dreams only a golfer can understand and enjoy. I think often of what Bobby Jones said when he first saw the old nursery he eventually transformed into Augusta National. "It seemed as though the land had sat here for centuries, waiting for a golf course to be put upon it."

Quiz time

Can you guess the sport? You check in and they hand you a score-card. They may ask for your credit card. You put on special shoes, then play the game without knowing or meeting the people playing all around you. You get in the car and leave, thinking maybe you'll do this again someday and maybe you won't.

If you guessed bowling—or resort-course golf—hop to the head of the class.

The kind of courses pros like

Tour pros are discouraged from publicly criticizing the courses they play. The PGA Tour's reasoning is similar to the NBA not allowing players to lambaste the referees—it makes the whole product look bad. But for the record, there are certain courses players don't like. Usually it's because of one or two holes.

Players don't like courses with holes where they can make a huge number. A guy who's worked all week to get near the lead on Sunday, and who has a wife and three kids to feed at home, doesn't like seeing the whole store fly out the window because of one bad swing. He'll accept a double-bogey if it's induced by a truly horrible shot, but what he doesn't like is when a marginally bad shot leads to the double-bogey, and then a second so-so shot that turns the double into a quad.

A poor player will never
be transformed by
equipment. It may hide
his mistakes, but it
won't make him
a better player.

That's why I'm surprised there isn't more moaning about the par-3 seventeenth hole at the TPC at Sawgrass. I think a lot of the players secretly hate that hole, not because it can knock a guy out of the lead, but because it can knock him from first place to thirtieth in the space of two minutes. Mark my words, there is going to come a Sunday when the wind in Jacksonville is blowing forty miles per hour and hitting that green becomes next to impossible. The poor commissioner is going to be in the clubhouse next to the television, his face in his hands.

OUR NEWEST SUPERSTARS

Teachers then and now

When Byron Nelson, Ben Hogan, Dr. Cary Middlecoff, I, and the rest of us needed help, we turned to each other. When I was a boy, the dinner table at the Burke home was an informal classroom where well-known players would stop by to talk golf with my father. Years later, when I became a touring pro, the hotel rooms on summer nights were unbearably hot, so ten or twenty of us would spend hours in the lobby telling stories, discussing swing theory, and even giving informal lessons. We consulted each other on practice ranges and gabbed about the swing on the long car rides from tournament to tournament.

There was no other recourse but to help each other, because when I took up golf there was no such thing as a teaching pro. The club pro gave lessons, but never exclusively. He was too busy running the shop to teach full-time. There were a few men who specialized in studying the golf swing and who wrote about it a lot—Percy Boomer, Alex Morrison, and Ernest Jones come to mind—but nobody tried to make a living at teaching. Even in the 1980s, there were very few full-time teachers.

The moral of the story is: There were still many great players.

Can your guru play?

When I spent summers teaching, I made it a point to practice my own game for an hour and a half every day. It gave my teaching a much-needed boost. See, no one takes up the game wanting to be a teacher. They don't say, at age twelve, "I want to be Tiger Woods's teacher someday." No, they want to be players. They only resort to teaching when they discover they can't make a living playing. That's all right, but teachers should certainly continue to play regularly and be able to play pretty darned well. It shows they've devoted years to trying to figure this hard game out, and have acquired empathy for what the student experiences.

Beginner teachers

I gave my first lessons when I was thirteen years old. By that age I had consumed a tremendous amount of information, having listened to Jack Grout, Harvey Penick, John Bredemus, Byron Nelson, Ben Hogan, and the rest talk golf at our house for hours on end. I was developing into a pretty good little player, and because of that the members at River Oaks, where my dad was the head pro, would call me over to look at their swings.

At thirteen I did exactly what every poor teacher does to this day, which is give out as much information as possible so the pupil would think he was getting his money's worth. I still believe that if a teacher tells you about the grip, stance, backswing, and forward swing in the space of one hour and never stops talking except for the

Clubfitting helps. But if you hand a good player a club right off the store-room shelf, after five swings he'll hit it almost as well as his own club.

two seconds when you're actually hitting a ball, you should head for the exits. You might as well just learn on your own, because there's no way the human brain can assimilate all that information.

Dr. Answerall

Sometimes I tune in to the Golf Channel and watch the show where the folks at home call in to the studio and ask a guest teacher for help. The instructors have one hard and fast rule, I think, and it's to answer the question, no matter how hard it is. That's important to establish their knowledge and authority. A poor lady from Kansas will say she's hitting her driver to the right half the time and to the left the rest of the time, and what is she doing wrong? The guest teacher will tell her it's her swing path or that her clubface is open or closed, or that her stance is too wide or narrow. It's pretty clear he's grasping at straws.

Here's the answer they should give half the time: "I don't know. I'd really have to spend some time with you on the range to answer that question." That would be the responsible thing to say. He could suggest that the lady from Kansas visit her local PGA pro.

But they can't do it. They feel they have to say *something*. These instructors are all variations of the same person. He's known as "Dr. Answerall," and he prescribes answers without really knowing the question. But Dr. Answerall has no trophies, no accomplishments to back up his supposed wealth of knowledge.

That poor cat

Good teachers make teaching look easy. Bad ones approach it like they're haphazardly dissecting a cat. They address every single movement possible, and by the time they're done they've taken apart the entire cat. There's blood and guts everywhere, but where is the cat? Every person comes to the teacher with his own distinctive swing, and it's up to the teacher to improve on what the student has, not build a new swing from the ground up. I'll always believe that teaching is an art. Good instructors measure the person's intellect, athleticism, experience, and talent before they say anything. They then tailor the lessons to the individual. Just as every person draws the letter "A" a little differently, each person needs a different program, a time frame for improving, and a method for getting the message.

The man with the pipe

By the time I came back from World War II and took a job at Metropolis Country Club in New York, my teaching had come a long way. I had matured. I had begun to understand how difficult learning was, and how most people can only absorb a bit of information at a time. I had to become more patient, knowledgeable, and creative. Some of my students showed real improvement. My own playing skills hadn't yet evolved to where I could make a decent portion of my income through playing, but my ability as a teacher strengthened my confidence that I could obtain a club pro position at a good club.

Late one summer, one of the members at Metropolis fell into a terrific bout of shanking. The vexing thing was, he shanked only chip shots, nothing else. It was due to his taking an exaggerated out-to-in swipe across the ball. He finally came to me feeling totally humiliated. The day before he had shanked a series of chips, his ball shooting off at a ninety-degree angle each time, until he had traveled in a complete circle around one of the greens. The other members had teased him mercilessly. I've never seen a man more desperate for help; he offered to pay me any amount of money if I could end his waking nightmare.

The man smoked a pipe. After a lot of thought, I placed his best pipe just outside his ball. He was terrified of hitting the pipe with the toe of the club, you see, so he stopped swinging out-to-in. I cured him quick.

I was telling this story in Houston not long ago and a member overheard it and disappeared. He came back an hour later and placed his pipe, which was shattered to bits, in front of me. "Your tip doesn't work for long irons," he said.

The toughest student

Teachers have a tough job when they take on a student who is out to dominate the game. Some people are so intent on getting better *right now* that they can't accept the teaching process. They don't have the patience for it. They want to master each segment quickly and then move on to the next point. They view it almost like the martial arts, where you earn different colored belts in succession. But to get your black belt in golf, you often have to put the red belt back on for a while. To learn to hit a flop shot, you may have to re-visit the fundamentals of grip pressure for a day to reinforce the role of soft hands in executing that shot. A bit of regression is necessary to let an advanced point sink in. It's a tough game no matter how good you get. Why did Tiger Woods practice for six hours yesterday? Because he knows he will never dominate the playing of this game.

You may hit your 8-iron close to the hole four times in one round, but that doesn't mean you've mastered the 8-iron, because tomorrow it might be ten degrees colder, the wind will have changed direction, and you are three pounds lighter. Everything has changed. Herodotus said, "A man never crosses the same river twice, because the river has changed and so has the man." Boy, is that ever true in golf.

The camera is never wrong

I'm very suspicious of video cameras. On one hand, pictures don't lie and there is some value in being able to show a student where his club is during the swing or some such thing. But there is so much else the camera doesn't show. The camera can't photograph what's in a player's brain. It doesn't show what he sees in his mind's eye. It doesn't reveal temperament, timing, or what the player feels.

The camera is only a tool, an adjunct. Remember the primitive hunter? He didn't line up his spear by looking at his reflection in a lake. He learned to be perceptive, to use his instincts and intuition. He didn't do what modern teachers do—examine a photograph of the clubface midway through the backswing and then draw lines on it. If the primitive hunter did those things, he'd be dinner.

The problem with "tips"

I am wary of things called "tips." Not long ago, a member at Champions asked me to have a quick look at his swing. I agreed and offered a short suggestion. As he walked away, he exclaimed, "Thanks for the tip!"

I don't give tips. This isn't Churchill Downs. It took me sixty years to acquire the knowledge necessary to offer that man a suggestion. Just because the advice comprises one sentence doesn't mean it didn't include a lot of thought. I only gave it when I knew

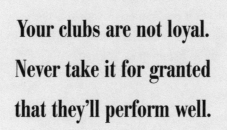

Your clubs are not loyal.

Never take it for granted

that they'll perform well.

the advice would fit in well with the rest of his swing. I forced a smile and told the fellow, "Glad you liked the *tip*. Come back in five years and I'll give you another one."

Don't ask, don't tell

Teachers entertain too many questions from their students, beginners especially. I don't usually care to be interviewed by my students. I don't like them asking questions until they are far enough along to ask the right questions. That may sound harsh, but as I see it, answering your question won't do you much good, because it's rarely relevant to what I'm trying to do with you. It just slows things down. If you've got confidence in your teacher, show him the same respect you would a teacher in school and listen up. You should do ten times as much listening as talking.

Not for hire

I enjoy helping tour players with their short games and don't mind giving a little input on their full swings. As for becoming a full-time guru, forget it. I don't want a tour pro phoning me in the middle of the night, or referring to me as "coach." That sort of dependence is the last thing I need. And it's the last thing *they* need.

So many players, even top professionals, would profit by learning to diagnose their own problems. You need to be independent and figure things out for yourself.

This isn't to say a player shouldn't visit his instructor now and again to review the basic things they've been working on. Working on a major swing change during the off-season sometimes makes sense as well. But the idea of an instructor flying into a tour event on Thursday for a fifteen-minute lesson before a Friday tee time boggles my mind. That player will never be all he can be.

What a way to go

Have you seen all the contraptions teachers use these days? Straps, belts, harnesses, mirrors, clubs with gizmos attached to them, jackets, balls with stripes on them, special glasses, you name it. If I manufactured those things I'd be worried. It's only a matter of time before someone hangs himself with one of them.

CHAPTER TWO

WHEAT FIELD OR BATTLEFIELD?

A PLEA FOR MORE AMATEUR COMPETITION

In Houston there is a unique group of golfers known as the Medalist Golf Association. The group is comprised of about 250 members and operates independently of any club or official organization. Six times a year, its members throw some money into a pot, purchase the use of a golf course for two consecutive mornings, and conduct a thirty-six-hole tournament. To keep costs down, there are no gift bags or much in the way of merchandise prizes. Instead, the winner of each event is awarded a simple red head cover, which he displays on his driver until the conclusion of the next tournament, when a new winner takes possession of the "trophy." The men have a sandwich when play is concluded each day, talk golf for a while, and then go home or back to work.

The red head cover carries a good deal of prestige because the Medalist has an uncommonly high standard of play. Their one criterion for membership is that a player carry a handicap of 5 or lower. The founding fathers, of whom my son, Mike, is one, put that rule in place due to their dissatisfaction with the competitions conducted at their respective clubs. There are tournaments, to be sure, but

A golf club filled with high-handicap players is like a yacht club where nobody can sail a boat.

virtually all them are low-net affairs played with handicaps. Members of the Medalist have a singular view of competition. They like it raw and honest, with no advantage given to anyone in order to make it "fair." To a man, these fellows would rather lose a hard-fought match to another good player than win a resounding victory over someone they were giving a handful of strokes. As they see it, no-strokes competition is more gratifying, win or lose, than "jolly golf" played with handicap strokes. It means more to them, for the same fundamental reason Tiger Woods is more fulfilled by winning the U.S. Open than he would be by winning the Oldsmobile Scramble.

I realize that a relatively small percentage of golfers carry handicaps of 5 or better, and that a world comprised only of them would be a small world indeed. Still, the fact that strong amateur golf competition is so scarce that the Medalist has to operate anonymously and independently of the mainstream is tragic to me. It shows that we don't appreciate top amateur competition, either as spectators or, more alarmingly, as participants. There's a general apathy toward it, a sense it isn't worthwhile and runs contrary to the essential purpose of a club—relaxation and escape from the competitive rigors of everyday life. In fact, I believe competition and relaxation go hand in hand. The more you promote competition, the more relaxing and enjoyable the atmosphere becomes.

To relax, you must compete

There are many forms of relaxation. Listening to music, reading, and engaging in a hobby are favorites, because they involve total immersion in the subject. "Getting lost" in a pastime is deeply fulfilling to those who have learned the art of doing it.

I've always viewed competition as the deepest type of immersion into the game. Whenever an important match or tournament came to an end, I was amazed by the tremendous sense of calm and satisfaction I felt. It was almost as though I had been in a trance. I realized early on that there was no other way to get the most that golf had to offer than to compete. Just knowing that I was in the fray and doing the very best I could seemed to answer the question as to what the game was all about. I think my discovery would ring true with everyone. If you avoid competing, it doesn't wear well with the idea of taking up the game in the first place. I mean, the scorecard is there for a reason. It you dislike competition, why did you join a club?

Just entering a competition (and yes, a low-net event will fill the bill) will do a lot for you. Nothing—not the nice car, big house, or other material amenities associated with affluent "country club" living—will give you as much satisfaction.

The win/lose dichotomy

You may not realize it, but we Americans compete every day. It's the story of our lives. Whether it's at the job, arguing our way out of a traffic ticket, or trying to get the last toy off the shelf at a Christmas sale, we compete. It's natural to us. Yet the idea of competing at golf terrifies many people.

To those who harbor a fear of competition, I'd like to point out that scoreboards are everywhere. They're on your bank statement, your paycheck, and on your bathroom scale. We see them every single day. The ones at the golf course are different only in that they have no consequence except as it applies to the game.

Some golfers carry an inordinate fear of losing and thus avoid the fray altogether. This is tragic, for if you're a golfer and have never won or lost in a serious competition, you're just treading water. You really don't know where the deep end of the pool is. It's a terrible world to live in. The only way to feel any real sense of accomplishment is to post a score. Even a poor score will fulfill you if you did your best.

Those who take a chance at competing learn very quickly that people do not think less of them if they fail. Regardless of what they say or how much they tease you, deep down they respect and admire you for trying.

Consecrating the field of play

If you take a wheat field and do nothing but grow crops on it, it will forever be a wheat field. But if a war is fought on it, it becomes a battlefield. Suddenly it stands for something. The sacrifice, effort, and spirit expended there transform it from an ordinary piece of land into something remarkable.

The best golf courses are similar. Augusta National, Shinnecock Hills, Oakmont, and Southern Hills are hallowed places. As golfers we admire them, wonder about them, and yearn to see them because they have been consecrated by the efforts of competitive people who put their pride, skill, and courage on the line. Dramatic events transpired there, events that will be remembered forever. They are beautiful places, to be sure, but it's the competition that makes them stand apart from hundreds of places like them. No matter how hard you try, low-net competitions, 200 millionaires as members, and a ten-year waiting list won't turn any golf course into a battlefield.

From the day Jimmy Demaret and I founded Champions Golf Club, we wanted it to be special. There was only one surefire way to ensure that it would stand out, and it had nothing to do with the name of the architect, how much money we spent, or the size of a prospective member's checkbook. We knew that serious competition, nationally and especially locally, would make the club a place people would gravitate toward. It would instill in everyone connected with it a sense of real pride. It has been my aim to give Houstonians and the world a taste of what serious competition is about, and demonstrate it continually.

To a large extent, our success in staging a U.S. Open, the U.S. Amateur, the Ryder Cup, several Tour Championships, and many other prominent competitions is only part of what makes Champions distinctive. The biggest part is our effort to promote grass-roots amateur competition every single day. To be a member, you have to have a handicap of 15 or better. At this writing we have 270 members who have handicaps of 5 or better, more than any other club in America. We also have a unique club championship. Played over the Labor Day weekend, the low fifteen qualifiers plus the defending champion go at it in as intense a display of match play as you will ever see. It culminates in a thirty-six-hole final. A big gallery shows up to watch. The interest is intense, almost like a small tour event.

The amateur's greatest gift

When good players are at the course, everyone is inspired to raise their games a notch. The sight of a skilled foursome of golfers striding purposefully off the first tee makes everyone's heart beat a little faster. The good players inspire youngsters to imitate them—what golfer can't recall having a local club hero when they were young? Good players are an asset to any club or course. They add immeasurably to the atmosphere. Usually the top players are aware of

The day you stop competing is the day you start the long walk to the graveyard.

their standing and live up to it in the way they dress, their behavior, their modesty, and their good sportsmanship. They set a positive tone for everyone.

The only way to promote any game, to make it better, is through competition. I have never seen a crowd gather around the worst players. They want to see the best in everything, because watching them not only entertains them, it inspires them to get better. Clubs that emphasize gimmicky competitions are trying to improve the game from the bottom up instead of from the top down.

A visit with Bobby Jones

During Masters week each year, the club hosts the Champions Dinner. Everybody who's won a green jacket is invited and we tell stories and have a good meal. It's a fine time for all of us, the only time many of us get to see each other.

Not many years after I won the 1956 Masters, I got to sit next to Bobby Jones. Jones, of course, was and is known as the quintessential amateur, the only truly great player who never turned pro. But I knew that Jones had made money through golf after his retirement, and assumed he'd forfeited his amateur status.

"So when did you turn pro?" I asked him.

Talk about terrible mistakes. Jones stared at me so long and hard I thought I'd turn to salt.

"I never turned professional," he said sternly.

"What about the books you wrote, the movies you made?" I asked. "Didn't you profit from them?"

Jones didn't give me much of an answer, though he made it clear he didn't like the question. He saw himself as a lifelong amateur. I later asked Joseph C. Dey, the executive director of the U.S. Golf

Association, why Jones wasn't considered a pro under the strict definition of the Rules of Amateur Status.

"Well, we've created a classification called *non-amateur*," Joe said. That took care of Bobby Jones's amateur status. But I didn't come away satisfied with that answer. You either make money off of your golf expertise or you don't. You're either a pro or you're not.

The eyes of others are upon you

To succeed at golf, you have to master the art of not being embarrassed. You have to take your ego out of the equation and just play. It's incredibly hard to erase thoughts of how you're going to be perceived by others, and the challenge never ceases. You think Arnold Palmer doesn't feel embarrassed when he yips a four-foot putt in front of a big gallery? Sure he does. He mastered the art of not being embarrassed years ago, and now he's learning it again.

Finding things that don't intimidate you is a full-time job. Most people are at least a bit frightened of many things. Golf can be intimidating, but you have to take it on. If you do that, you very soon won't be intimidated at all. There is enough truly scary stuff going on in the world that nothing connected to golf should be.

The non-competitor

Early man was a hunter. He discovered that if he didn't kill the rabbit, his family didn't eat. It's a very basic realization, and the desire to hunt was bred in us. It continues to this day, though there's a school of thought that it would be best if it were bred out of us.

The best competitors embrace the hunter vs. rabbit equation. Others look for a free plate of rabbits and have no desire whatsoever

If the thought of competing makes you nervous, remember this: Aim for the stage, not the audience.

to set the trap or pick up the bow and arrow. They are only hurting themselves. Eventually they will go hungry.

Fan factory

At all levels of sports there is a tremendous emphasis on winning. Even at the high school level, coaches are expected to produce decent results or else lose their jobs. The result is that only the best players make the team and get to play. That leaves a lot of kids with no recourse but to play trombone in the school band.

If the kid doesn't compete in high school, he certainly isn't going to play in college. Invariably he becomes—what else?—a fan. He likes sports, but his main experience has been as an observer, so that's the limit of his involvement. When he eventually builds a family, the children are less likely to receive a hands-on education in how to compete, and thus become fans as well. We've become a fan factory. This is one reason that a love of serious play is dying. Our citizens simply don't know how to compete.

The most tragic case

Most people who have been around golf awhile have witnessed the following case. An outstanding young player leaves college with a degree and a love of competition. He quickly finds he has nowhere to test himself other than at his state amateur and, if he can afford it, the U.S. Amateur. Because he's better by leaps and bounds than other amateurs in the vicinity and he thirsts for competition, he turns pro and tries playing a mini-tour you've never heard of. Two years later, after he's gone broke and failed his audition for "The Big Break," this nightmare draws to a close. The USGA reinstates his amateur status and he's back where he started, with no place to test his skill. He looks around and sees the PGA Tour on one end and low-net hit-and-giggles on the other end, with very little in between. Some happy ending for the good amateur player, who to me has always been the heart and soul of golf!

This is the most tragic case. When a young player comes to me in confidence and asks my opinion on whether he or she is good enough to play the PGA or LPGA Tour, I resort to the dialogue invented by Jimmy Demaret for just this occasion. Years ago, a kid asked Jimmy for his opinion on whether he was "ready" to play against the big boys on the PGA Tour.

Jimmy answered the question with a question. "Son, can you beat everybody in your home state?"

"No sir, I can't," said the boy.

"Then don't leave," said Jimmy. I think that's still pretty good advice.

Speech at the 2004 Champions Cup

The most significant amateur competition we conduct is the annual Champions Cup Invitational. Now in its thirty-eighth year, it consists of two-man teams from across America. To enter, the two players must be from the same state, and each player must have a handicap of 3 or better.

Most of the prestigious amateur tournaments in the U.S. are individual competitions. They include the U.S. Amateur, U.S. Mid-Amateur, Porter Cup, Northeast Amateur, Western Amateur, and a select few others. The Champions Cup is slightly different in that it's an invitational and a bit more relaxed. Like the Anderson Memorial played at Winged Foot, the Coleman Invitational at Seminole, and a few similar others, the players consider it something of an honor to be invited. There is more socializing, which is not to say the golf isn't serious once the battle is underway.

Six of the entrants in last year's Champions Cup are employed at Taylor Made, the equipment company, and they sent their club repair trailer here. For these serious golfers, it was an opportunity to be treated like tour pros. I don't know how many players had new grips installed, got a driver reshafted, or had a set of irons bent flatter or more upright, but the trailer sure was a busy place that week.

These are my kind of people. As tournament host, I always offer a few remarks at dinner the night before the competition begins. Here's what I had to say to the field in 2004:

Good evening. In a society of growing developer courses that resemble bowling alleys where you go in, get a scorecard, shoot a number, take the card with you, and leave—never to see the people again—you represent something else entirely. You all are good players, the heart and soul of the game.

My message tonight is short and simple. You can dance around the game, eat around it, and sell products around it, but at the end of the day somebody has to play and compete. The amateur game needs better players and more meaningful tournaments like this one.

Tournaments at most clubs were put in place by high-handicap players who chose to serve on the board, and they tend to deliver tournaments to suit their brand of golf. Unfortunately, we have hundreds of colleges turning out players of high quality who are not being absorbed well into the mainstream of American golf. The quality of play is not representative of their ability. This has to change. Since the USGA remains on the East Coast and doesn't get out here much, amateurs like you find they are on their own. But this week is something special. So let's get after it!

No help from the gate-clangers

Many state golf associations are faced with a strange, almost unbelievable problem. When it comes time to line up sites for important state amateur competitions, associations have found that many clubs are unwilling to give up their courses for a week. These clubs invariably are extremely well financed and their courses are among the best, which is why they are sought as venues for competition. But the members at these clubs are against such competitions because it means closing the course for a week. To these members, the attention and adulation the club receives doesn't outweigh the fact that they won't have a place to play for seven days.

I call such members "gate clangers." They post the guards at the entrance and won't let anybody in. They give golf a bad name. The worst of them are perversely proud of the way they reject entreaties to stage tournaments. "We don't need the attention," they sniff. Gate-clanging clubs usually are filled with members who can't play worth a damn and really don't have golf in their souls. They expect nothing from the game, and to ensure that the arrangement is fair, they give nothing to it.

It is best to let the gate clangers have their way. As a private club, it is their right to manage their organization any way they see fit. The down side is that these clubs will never be all they can be. They have the illusion they are something special, but in truth they are little more than wheat fields.

Scrambles are all right
once in a while. But they
remind me of a game of
tag where no one is "it."

Exception to the rule

There is a notion going around that golf is a game everyone can play. I suppose it's possible for everyone to give it a try, but not everyone is cut out for it, just as some people aren't suited for chess or fencing. Maybe golf needs a softer sell.

Most clubs have some members who socialize a lot but only play a couple of times a year. For them the game truly is a good walk spoiled. Why is that? In a lot of cases they took up the game with some very wrong assumptions. They figured they would pick up the game quickly and learn to play it as effortlessly as Harry Connick, Jr., plays the piano, and it just isn't possible. That realization hits them hard, and if it so happens they are extremely uncoordinated to boot, the game is drudgery. In some cases they would be well advised to take up another game. To play the game even remotely well requires some sense of balance, coordination, strength, and an ability to throw. Some human beings just can't do that, and golf is a tough game for them.

The up side is they don't take any divots.

CHAPTER THREE

THE GOLF SWING

HOW TO MAKE THE HARD LOOK EASY

A golfer friend of mine tells me of the time he went into downtown Houston to pick up a friend for lunch. When he arrived at the man's office several minutes early, the fellow's secretary explained that her boss was in a meeting but would be out shortly. She invited my friend to wait in the man's personal office.

As my friend waited, he couldn't help but survey the room. It was spacious and comfortable, with nice carpeting, wood-paneled walls, and a large window looking out to the north. A high-backed leather chair sat behind a huge oak desk. On the desk was a handsome clock, a new ink blotter, a few documents, and two fresh pencils sitting beside a yellow legal pad. The occupant was obviously a golfer; a pen-and-pencil caddy set with a golf ball perched in the middle—a prize for winning a local pro-am—was close at hand.

But the item on the desk that really caught his eye was a small wood carving of a hunting dog, an Irish setter. It appeared to be original, not store-bought. The detail was fantastic, from the hair-lined texture of the dog's coat to the graceful bend in the dog's foreleg. The fact that the dog's tail was slightly out of proportion was the

41

only clue that the carving was done by a hobbyist rather than a professional sculptor. He envied it.

When the owner of the office appeared a few minutes later, my friend immediately asked about the carving. "Where did you get that?" he asked. "I couldn't take my eyes off that thing."

"You like it?" the man said proudly. "I made it myself,"

The guest was impressed. "How did you go about making it?"

"It was easy," the man said, grabbing his coat. "I got a very sharp knife and a clean block of wood. Then I cut away everything that didn't look like a dog."

Creating a good golf swing is exactly like carving that dog. No two swings should be alike because no two people are alike physically, emotionally, or temperamentally. After the extraneous movements are removed, the swing will reveal itself as a work of art, a motion as natural as walking and as distinctive as a fingerprint. You don't need a computer, a blueprint, or a biomechanical model to make one. Just as every athlete throws a baseball or shoots a basketball a bit differently, so it is with your swing. It should reflect your personality and a bit of your heart and soul.

Do I know you?

I sometimes travel to Miami to assist my friend Jim McLean with the successful golf school he runs at Doral Golf Resort. I've known Jim since he was in college at the University of Houston. Today he's one of the best teachers in the world, but I remember him as an inquisitive young man who always seemed to have a pencil and notepad with him. He's the note-takingest son of a gun I've ever seen. These days, Jim likes it when I come to Florida and talk to his students about the golf swing. I like it, too. It's an enjoyable diversion and helps keep me sharp.

During a recent visit to Doral, one of Jim's students approached me seeking advice on a commercial venture he was eager to get underway. He had found some rare footage of top pros of the 1940s which he hoped to compile and make available commercially. He was especially enamored with Ben Hogan, and was sure that his hero was among the many players captured on film. He wanted me to watch the film and identify the players.

The film wasn't of the best quality, but nevertheless I was able to name every player. Craig Wood, Claude Harmon, and many others were recognizable, not by their faces or dress but by their swings. Even after sixty years, there was no mistaking the nuances of each player. Sadly for the man at Doral, only part of the film I saw contained images of Ben Hogan.

I sometimes feel that if many modern instructors had their way, every player would look alike. These teachers believe there is a "correct" way of swinging the club that would make every golfer a carbon copy. Although they are sincere in their efforts to help golfers improve, I can't say I go along with their regimented, systematic approach to teaching. I like the fact that I can look out at the far end of Champions' double-ended practice range and recognize members just by their swings. They are as identifiable to me by their swings as Bing Crosby is by hearing his voice. If I played golf with you tomorrow and a year passed before your next visit, I might not remember your name, but I would remember your swing.

My father liked to say, "The only system is one where there is no system." After playing, teaching, and observing golf for the better

**At no time in the
backswing does the back
of your left hand face the
ground.**

part of my eighty-three years, I've seen nothing to convince me otherwise.

The gift of strong hands

My dad, who finished second in the 1920 U.S. Open, wasn't certain I should try to play golf for a living. He didn't think my hands were strong enough to take the continual pounding of practicing and playing all the time. Dad was perceptive, and he turned out to be right. When I turned pro I had to practice a lot to maintain my timing because my hands weren't strong enough to maneuver the club without some conscious effort. My hands really took a pounding. I envied Jimmy Demaret, who had large durable hands with fingers like big cigars. Jimmy could go two weeks without playing and come back as good as ever. From all that practicing I developed tendonitis and had to withdraw from a lot of tournaments, especially late in my career after I won the PGA Championship and Masters in 1956.

I succeeded in spite of my "handicap." My hands weren't strong, but they were sensitive. Good touch will take you a long way.

The case for the ten-finger grip

If I were starting over today, I might personally use the ten-finger grip. I have a hunch it will grow in popularity when golfers and their teachers see how beneficial it can be. No question, it's the best grip if your hands are small or weak—it's wonderful for women, children, and seniors. It's also good for men with thick hands and stubby fingers. With all ten fingers on the club, your hands and wrists are more pliable and hinge more easily. Your right hand will be placed a fraction lower on the handle, which gives you more ıeverage, much as you place one hand well below the other when using a shovel or rake.

The ten-finger grip is a tough sell in view of the fact that no great player in recent history has used it. A larger point I'd like to make is that you don't want to teach everyone the same grip. A child can't grip the club the way an adult does because his hands are weak and his fingers are short. Children, women, and weaker men will instinctively grasp the club with all ten fingers on the club, as though they're holding a baseball bat. Their grips are usually "strong," or rotated to the right, to help them get a little more leverage. Don't correct them. They're trying to bring the hands into play. Let them, and weaken the grip as they get older and stronger.

Like sqeezing water from a towel

The grip is the most important fundamental in golf. With that, I'm a bit more flexible than my teaching colleagues about adhering to a model grip. Experience has shown me it's possible to be successful with any number of styles. Ed Fiori, who went to the University of Houston and won some PGA Tour events, had such a strong grip—his right hand was rotated well under the handle—that his nickname was "The Grip." There are many anomalies like Ed and several sound, fundamental styles, too. I've come to believe that exercising some personal preference is fine, so long as you obey a few basic principles and don't allow your grip to impede your ability to transport the club.

The single most important rule is to use your fingers to press the handle into your palms. Start by holding the club vertically in front of you, the handle twelve inches from your chest and the club-head aimed at the sky. Your hands should be open so part of the handle is exposed. The handle should be positioned very loosely in the fingers of both hands, which have yet to close around the handle.

Now close your fingers around the handle, pressing it into your palms as you do so. The grip is now complete and you can lower the club behind the ball.

The whole process is similar to squeezing water from a small towel—you place the wet towel in your fingers, both hands grasping it at once, and press the towel into the palms with your fingers so you can squeeze the water from it efficiently. You don't want to wring the towel dry, only squeeze the excess water from it.

Eating vs. log carrying

Ben Hogan felt that your forearms should be close together at address and remain that way throughout the swing. In his *Five Lessons* instruction book, he illustrated this with a drawing of his arms actually banded together. He liked the tips of the elbows pointing at his hip joints at address, the inner portion of the forearms facing the sky. He felt your arms should be kept directly in front of you at all times.

I never agreed with Ben on this point. To me, the arms-close position suggested someone carrying an armful of logs into a cabin to put on the fireplace. Bunching your arms together at address seemed unnatural and unnecessary. After all, on the downswing, centrifugal force will straighten your arms in front of you and bring them sufficiently close together to swing the club through the ball with plenty of speed and accuracy.

I always felt that wielding a golf club should be similar to holding a knife and fork at mealtime. What's more natural than eating?

In that instance, your upper arms are just forward from the sides of your body. Your forearms, though in front of you, are facing each other and aren't particularly close together. From this position, you have the freedom to reach for the salt shaker across the table. In golf, you'll take the club away from the ball better, a bit to the inside. And your arms will have all the room they need to swing freely coming down.

Hogan's 500 fundamentals

I don't want to criticize Ben without giving him some praise, too. Over the years I've heard him describe hundreds of swing thoughts and ideas he was working on at a given moment. Each one of these ideas was extremely important to him at the time. They began as experiments, but if they merited inclusion in his swing, they became fundamentals to him. For example, he adjusted the position of his right foot constantly. Depending on what he was doing with his swing, his foot would be turned in or out a bit at address. He must have had 500 fundamentals like that, some of which he used for his entire career, some of which lasted only a week or a day, and others that didn't make it past the practice range. I tend to believe the "fundamentals" he described in his book were not as etched in stone as he implied.

The adjustments Ben made were, above all else, *his* fundamentals. He understood that every golfer is different. A fundamental is simply an idea that works for you. It may or may not have something to do with your grip, stance, or address position. It is merely something that is so critical that you're a markedly better player when you use it. That fundamental may be pointing the shaft at the target

Late in the downswing, try
to extend your arms. They
should feel like they are
straining to leave your
shoulder sockets.

at the top of the backswing. It may be holding the club more lightly with the right hand than the left.

You don't need to adhere to fundamentals the way another person—even Ben Hogan—has defined them.

Aim vs. alignment

I encourage you to take lessons from your PGA professional. But if the first thing he does is lay clubs on the ground and tell you to place your feet squarely to one of them, head for the exits. Alignment is overrated. If Lee Trevino placed his feet square instead of open (to the left of the target), or if Bobby Locke had set up square instead of closed (to the right), we never would have heard of either of them. I believe you line up your feet and shoulders in a way that best allows you to deliver the clubhead squarely into the ball from inside the line of play. If a golfer has difficulty pivoting fully, a closed stance can lengthen his turn and help him swing from the inside.

Aim is much more important than alignment. Aim is all about the clubface. That's why my friend Harvey Penick's watchwords were "Take dead aim." Harvey was so right. On every shot, identify the target and then burn your eyes into that clubface to make sure it's aimed precisely.

Roll out the barrel

Some years ago, the trend in teaching was to inject a fair amount of lateral motion into the swing. When Curtis Strange was winning U.S. Opens, photographs indicated his head and upper body moved well to his right on the backswing. Teachers really picked up on that and noted that the swing was a combination of lateral and rotary motion. Technically speaking, they were right—photographs don't lie—but I didn't see many golfers improve by suddenly trying to move the head eight inches to the right and then back to the left on the downswing. As if this game isn't complicated enough!

The golf swing is a rotary motion, period. Surely you want to shift your weight to the right and then back to the left, but the lateral movement occurs by way of pivoting, not sliding. When you turn your hips and shoulders, the distribution of weight will naturally move in the direction in which you're turning. On the backswing, about 80 percent of your weight will fall onto your right side. On the downswing, it moves back to the left.

I liken the motion on the backswing to moving a large barrel to your right. Now, you can't slide the barrel sideways without moving your feet because it's too heavy. Instead you lean the barrel on its side toward you, then you roll it to your right by pivoting your shoulders and hips.

Think about that. Your head will move marginally to your right because the top of your spine moves as you rotate your shoulders. But there is no conscious effort to slide sideways.

The importance of balance

Stand on your right leg. Now lift your left foot and see if you can tie your left shoe without hopping around or having to put your left foot back on the ground. If you can do that, you've got excellent balance. If you can't, you should know that balance is a make or break factor in golf. We all start out balanced when we address the ball, but not many of us have the ability to maintain balance throughout the swing. Imagine having to make a swing while standing on a steel girder five stories up in the air. I doubt you'd swing very violently. I think you'd make every effort to swing slowly with good rhythm. I believe it would dawn on you that the bottoms of your feet don't take up a lot of space and aren't much of a platform for a fellow who is six feet tall and weighs 194 pounds.

Some people are born with good balance. Leo Diegel, an outstanding player of the 1920s and 1930s, could shoot par standing on his left foot only. But balance can be learned. Put yourself on that imaginary steel girder. Get two clubs—old ones—and lay them on the ground so they are stance-width apart and run parallel to each other. Now stand on them so the shafts run beyond your heels and toes. Hit some balls this way, imagining that if either foot leaves either shaft, you'll plunge five stories down. This will teach you what balance is all about and will smooth out your swing in a hurry.

Turn the right shoulder first

The way you start the backswing is important and many players never do get it right. Unlike a lot of other sports, golf is started from a static position. It's difficult to start the swing in a way that allows you to arrive at the good positions you want at the top of the backswing.

Start the backswing by turning your right shoulder behind you. Don't try to turn your left shoulder under your chin, as it has too far to go to be very effective. It's very tempting to take the club away with the left side of your body, but it sets the stage for a lot of mistakes. The worst one is a sway, where you slide your body sideways to the right and destroy your pivot. You lose your power, leverage, and timing.

If you turn your right shoulder, you'll rotate your body instead of swaying. You'll make a big, pretty turn and all the pieces will fall into place. Don't worry about the left shoulder—it will follow the right; it has to. If you turn the right shoulder, you'll have a swing to die for.

Make a hard thing look easy

One reason golf is so captivating is that the best players make it look so simple and effortless. Ernie Els is nicknamed "The Big Easy" because his swing is rhythmic and unhurried, his muscles soft and relaxed. Whether he's driving the ball 320 yards or hitting a 9-iron 150, his swings tend to look alike. He exudes an air of low stress and drowsy calm.

The secret to Els's swing is balance. I'm sorry to ring the bell on balance again, but it's a fact. Imagine if he were asked to complete his swing in two-thirds the time it takes him now. I'll bet you'd see Ernie stumble for the first time in his life. I firmly believe that if you can swing without falling off balance, it will look simple and effortless. Even a funny swing can look easy. Your swing should look smooth and steady and never suggest violence. Try to make it feel as natural as water flowing out of a pipe.

Try "softer"

The smooth swing of a top professional is confounding to the average golfer. The poor fellow instinctively tries to copy the distance a pro gets by expending as much physical effort as possible. He gets so little for his effort and doesn't understand why. The game just doesn't seem to mirror everyday life. If hard work and thorough study offer rewards in other walks of life, why can't more effort supply an extra fifteen yards?

Golf is a game of opposites. You hit down to make the ball go up, swing left to make the ball curve right. Golf's contrary nature

The challenge of the grip
is to keep your hands firm,
but your wrists loose.

applies to every facet of the game, especially your bas'
of what the swing is about. The "softer" you try, the easi.
becomes. You learn faster and play better. Who hasn't swung easily
and been amazed at how far and straight the ball goes? Who hasn't
had days where every putt seems to drop, even when you pay less
attention to the line and your stroke than usual?

From this point forward, emulate Ernie Els's approach to the
swing. Adopt his low-stress demeanor in the way you learn the
game and make your swing. Leave your mind open and don't get so
balled up that you can't think or relax completely when you make a
swing. If you can't get around the notion that the game is enor-
mously difficult and complex, at least try to pretend the game is
easy. Let the game come to you instead of attacking it with such in-
tensity and fervor. You'll be surprised at how quickly things fall into
place.

Learn to let go

You can learn a lot by watching a small child play on a swing in the
park. The parent gets the child started by making sure the child is
seated firmly. Then the parent draws the swing away until the child
is nice and high. At that point the parent just lets go.

The golf swing is the same way. After you reach the top, let grav-
ity take over. You don't need a sudden push to get the downswing
started; that will, in fact, ruin your timing. Let your speed and
power accumulate gradually.

Happy landings

The thing that makes the kid in the swing squeal is the feeling of
being out of control. One of the essential appeals of swinging a club

is that it's free and a little reckless. We love the reward of reckless-ness, which is watching the ball fly a long way. Golf is partly about control, but one of the ironies is that to be in control, you have to be slightly out of control. If you allow the club to tear through the air with lots of speed, you'll have a better chance of hitting the ball far and straight than if you deliberately slowed your swing down and guided the club into the ball.

Being out of control on purpose and succeeding, and looking forward to being reckless again tomorrow, is a wonderful thing. The thrill is similar to sky diving—the parachute is packed carefully, you've been well trained, and the pilot knows what he's doing, but it doesn't mitigate the exhilaration of flying freely through the air.

Please don't interrupt

There are a hundred ways to interrupt a golf swing, and I don't mean someone coughing at the top of your backswing. The kind of interruptions I'm talking about are subtle and self-imposed. Do you ever contemplate the importance of a shot while you stand over the ball? Do you start the swing with more than one thought bouncing around inside your head? Those are interruptions. They kill any chance of making a continuous, fluid swing.

Allowing a mechanical thought to creep in after you take the club away from the ball disrupts your rhythm and timing. By inject-ing these thoughts into your swing, you end up not making a swing at all. Interruptions are like inserting a steering wheel on the down-swing. All spontaneity is lost. The picture you had in your mind vanishes. You end up consciously guiding the club into the ball in-stead of swinging freely through it.

I can't emphasize enough what a huge problem this is for the everyday player. You must remember that your last thought before you take the club away isn't a thought at all but a feeling, a sensation, a generalized vision of the swing as a whole. If you interrupt that with a conscious thought, you're gone.

How the hunter survived

The first athlete was the Stone Age hunter. You have to admire him. When he ventured into the jungle with only a crude spear, he either killed something or his family starved. So this fellow developed some serious skills. He used patience, stealth, alertness, experience, and intuition. When the primitive hunter threw a spear at his prey, there's no question he finished with his weight on his left foot and followed through. Reverse pivots back then could be fatal because the saber-tooth tiger was hungry, too. Any throwing motion requires a weight shift to the left. Stone Age man realized that. A million years later, poor golfers do not.

The forward part of the golf swing is a throwing motion, plain and simple. When you throw, your whole body gets in on the act. After you've coiled yourself, you uncoil your hips, rotate your shoulders, swing your arms, and uncock your wrists. You can't throw an object very far if your hips don't move. It's all fairly natural, and it doesn't do much good overthinking the process. Stone Age man was fairly unconcerned with swing plane. He just performed.

Oily ankles

It's imperative to be loose and relaxed during the swing. You hear it all the time. But I seldom hear specific comments about the knees, ankles, and feet. Looseness is very important there.

If you tighten your feet and ankles, you almost can't swing at all. It's amazing the chain reaction that takes place. The tension creeps upward into your knees, then your hips, and eventually your entire body. You can get totally frozen just by locking your ankles.

Your ankles should feel like you have oil in them. When you step into your address position, step lightly. Keep your feet sensitive enough to feel the firmness of the ground beneath you. If your feet and ankles are loose, your whole swing will show more freedom.

Lawson's lesson on timing

People forget what a fine player Lawson Little was. He won two U.S. Amateurs and two British Amateurs before deciding to turn pro. After that he won a U.S. Open. I traveled with Lawson for a time in my early days on tour. One year he gave a clinic at Pebble Beach during the Crosby. The subject was timing. First he shot his hands up in the air, telling the audience how fast they are. He wiggled his fingers and shook his hands to emphasize his point. "These are real fast," he said.

Then Lawson pointed to his stomach—he had a paunch—and said, "Now this is real slow. When I swing the club, I can't let these"—he shot his arms in the air again—"leave this [his stomach] behind."

Lawson was talking about timing. His point was that if you take the club back with your hands, your body never will catch up. On the backswing, I believe in taking your arms back slowly, so they trail your body slightly. On the downswing, the hands trail the body again. The hands and arms, which move fast, can never outrace your body. The inside governs the outside.

Finish the swing with the club on the back of your neck. If you can do that, you will always play to your satisfaction. Maybe not Hogan's satisfaction—nothing could satisfy him—but you'll do just fine.

ast news

one tries to determine what the hands should do during the critical moment when they deliver the clubhead into the ball. I've always likened the action to a farmer spreading seeds with his right hand. It's called "broadcasting." At the top of the backswing, imagine your right hand is filled with seeds. The palm faces toward the sky. On the downswing, you want to spread those seeds along the ground as evenly and over as wide a distance as you can. Through impact, you can only disperse the seeds properly if you maintain an angle in your right wrist. If you flip your right wrist too soon, those seeds will fly everywhere. You can throw the club as aggressively into the ball with your right hand as you wish, but you'll only get power and accuracy if you release the club as if you were broadcasting those seeds.

If the broadcasting analogy eludes you, imagine throwing rock salt on an ice-covered sidewalk. Again, this action will enable you to square the clubface naturally when it meets the ball. Note that broadcasting requires you to extend your hand farther away from you, as when you throw. Your right arm straightens as you release the seeds or rock salt.

Keep in mind what happens after the seeds are gone. As your hand moves across your body, the palm turns down and then moves around you. With a club in your hands, it means letting the clubhead travel back to the inside after the ball is gone.

Broadcasting works with every club in the bag, but it's especially important when hitting iron shots, because you're delivering a downward blow at the bottom of the ball.

The mud ball

My dad used to get water and dirt and make a ball of mud. He then would insert a stick into the ball of mud, and challenge his pupils to hurl it down the range. If the pupil released the stick too early— uncocked his wrists before it was time—the mud ball would leave the stick prematurely and rain mud everywhere. To fling the mud ball down the range, he had to maintain the angle in his right wrist through impact. The only way to throw the mud ball well was to start the forward motion slowly, and fling the stick late. It's another version of broadcasting, but with emphasis on beginning the down-swing in a leisurely way.

Toe up, toe down

When I was a kid, my dad taught me something very simple. He told me that the toe of the clubhead should point down at the top of the backswing, and point down again at the completion of my follow-through. If the two sides of your swing match up that way, it's very hard to play badly. It means that the clubhead is rotating naturally during the swing and is likely to be square at impact. I still like this reminder. If your arms are stiff, or you hold the club too tightly, the clubface won't open and close naturally. You have to keep your whole body soft and flexible, the arms and hands especially, for this to happen.

Strike a match

Because the ball is stationary, there's a common tendency to hit *at* the ball instead of *through* it. You want the club to be gaining speed as it passes through the ball, letting the momentum carry you to a full finish. It's like striking a match. You don't jab the head of a match into the matchbook, and the match sure as heck doesn't stop there. The idea is to drag the match, your fingers leading the way and the head of the match trailing behind. The matchstick is leaning to your left as you drag it across the abrasive strip on the matchbook.

The club is like a giant matchstick. Don't ignite the head suddenly. Use a long, even motion on the downswing and through impact, accelerating steadily. That's the way to set the ball on fire.

A fantastic finish

If you've got an awkward-looking follow-through, it means something went wrong earlier in the swing. Sometimes just improving your finish will take care of the problem that happened earlier. At the finish of the swing, I like to see the shaft on the back of your neck. Practice that. Make some practice swings and try to make the club whack you firmly on the back of your neck when the swing is complete.

How to nail it every time

The game is immeasurably easier if you know where the clubhead is. You need the same type of awareness as when you hammer a nail into a piece of wood. Hammering a nail is easy. Hitting a golf ball squarely isn't that difficult either.

Pretend the ball is divided into four sections, with a nail protruding from the quadrant nearest to your right foot. You want to hammer the nail straight through the ball with the face of the club. It's a good thought, a helpful way to strike the ball solidly with the clubhead approaching the ball from inside the target line.

Some muses from the old man

A little over a year before he passed away, my dad composed a list of thoughts on the golf swing. Some were eloquent and others more homespun, but they were sincere and reflected his core beliefs. Some years ago, my friend Robert McKinney published them in a small book called *Tips on the Game of Golf*.

Most of Dad's truisms hold up today. Some of the others I disagree with. I idolized my father, but I suppose I've put in enough hours teaching over the years to have earned the right to disagree with him.

Here are the tips from Jack Burke Sr., dated February 1, 1943, with my feelings as to their validity today.

- **The wrists play very little part in golf. The crossing of the forearms puts the punch in the golf shot.**
  True today. When you "broadcast the seeds" by uncocking your wrists through impact, you don't flip your hands. The wrists rotate more than they "flip."

- **The face of the club going off the line causes more poor shots than anything I know of.**
  True today. You want the clubface as square as possible as it travels down the line of play. You want it to travel down the target line as long as you can manage comfortably. Then it moves back inside the line of play.

- **If the club goes back properly, there isn't much chance of a bad shot.**
  Dad overstates the case here. He must have meant there's *less* chance of a bad shot. I've seen a lot of nice backswings produce poor shots, for lots of reasons.

it the ball in your mind and play the inside half. The
tside half should not be entertained.

True today, although I'd modify that to mean the inside *quadrant* of the ball instead of the inside *half.*

- **Learn to pick the ball clean—don't hoe it.**

  True today. I like very shallow divots with the irons. The way
  to do that is to turn your shoulders as level with the horizon
  as possible. If your left shoulder dips down abruptly on the
  backswing, your downswing will be too steep.

- **Picture a shot going perfectly to the line. It doesn't cost
  anything to give yourself the benefit of the doubt.**

  True today. What Dad is saying is have a positive picture of
  where you want the ball to go.

- **If the hands are severed together as one unit, one would
  be surprised by the amount of relaxation attained.**

  True today. I think by "severed together" he meant "joined
  together." Dad was a golf pro, not a college professor.

- **Knock the peg out from under the ball. This helps get
  the club through.**

  While true then, this one has become outdated. The ball was
  smaller back then, the tees shorter. You really tried to send
  the tee flying. Today, it's okay to dislodge the tee, but it
  doesn't hurt to leave it in place.

- **Let the ball get in the way of the swing instead of making
  the ball the object.**

This is just okay. I agree that you want to hit *through* and not *at* it, but at the same time you definitely want to keep your eyes riveted on the ball until it has taken flight.

- **Don't try to pick the ball up. The club is built for that purpose.**
  True today. The loft of the club gets the ball airborne.

- **Hitting behind the ball is caused by the weight being on the back foot. If the weight is forward, it would be impossible to hit behind the ball.**
  Unfortunately, there are many reasons for hitting the ball "fat," such as not keeping your hands ahead of the clubhead through impact. Dad's take on this may or may not apply to a given situation.

- **The reason for not going forward is tenseness. Keep the hands together and the move forward is easy.**
  True today. Everything you try to do with tenseness is tragic.

- **The more you try to get away from an object, the harder you hit it.**
  True today. What Dad is saying is when you want to hit something hard, you simply make a bigger turn "away" from it. If you're chopping down a tree, you obviously make a big, assertive turn.

- **Keep your feet moving to the line of flight. Don't let them freeze to the ground.**
  True today. As you shift your weight to the left and continue

into the downswing, feel like you're rolling your ankles to the left as well.

- **The shanked shot is caused by the club being on the outside of the ball. Put two balls together two inches apart—if you miss the outside ball, the shank is cured.**
  True today. One of the great shanking fixes of all time. You can shank by coming into the ball too much from the inside as well, but swinging out-to-in is much more common.

- **Have a little power left—don't put it all in the swing. You may need it before the game is over.**
  True today.

- **Let the club go where you expect the ball to go.**
  True today.

- **Finishing the swing is very important. Without a good finish, to keep the ball straight is luck.**
  True today. Remember what I said about the toe pointing down twice during the swing.

- **Get a system of some kind in playing. Any kind of system beats trusting to luck.**
  True today. Dad hated "systems" the way we describe them today, but he very much believed in sticking with a swing key if you're fortunate enough to stumble upon one.

- **Topping the ball is caused by closing the face of the club toward the body.**
  I believe the most common cause of topping is raising your left shoulder on the downswing.

- Slicing is caused by the hands leading the head of the club. Tenseness plays a major part. The face of the club is not flush at impact.

  There are many causes of slicing. This is only one of them.

- Learn to hook the ball rather than slice. Anyone slicing a ball has reached the top of his game—the harder he hits, the more he slices.

  Dad was being facetious when he said the slicer has reached the "top of his game." What he means is the slicer has reached rock bottom and won't improve without a wholesale change in his perception of what constitutes a good swing. In any case, it's true today!

- A ball lying badly: Better to try to pick it in preference to hoeing it out.

  That depends on how bad the lie is. If most of the ball is exposed, pick it. If it's buried, hoe it out. (Sorry, Dad.)

- Be honest with yourself. What you would find out in six months of practice your pro can tell you in five minutes.

  True today—Dad was drumming up business for his profession. Choose your teacher wisely.

- Hit the ball, then the ground. That will assure you of getting down to the ball.

  True today, tomorrow, and forevermore.

- Let the right hip take the club back and the left hip bring the club forward.

Dad loved Bobby Jones, and this is how Jones did it. It worked then and it works now.

- Try holding the right shoulder back as long as possible. This will give the left side a chance to get through.
  Works like a charm.

- Hold the head of the club off the ground if you are inclined to be tense.
  Jack Nicklaus, who came along after Dad was gone, always did this at address. It must work.

- Let the hands start slightly before the head of the club on the backswing.
  Another Bobby Jones technique. There are a number of ways to trigger the backswing, and this is a good one.

CHAPTER FOUR

LIFE AT THE CLUB

THE CARE AND FEEDING OF YOUR SECOND HOME

People join golf clubs because they're lonely.

Outwardly they might say it's because Champions has two outstanding eighteen-hole courses and a good practice facility. But the biggest reason has always been contact with other people. It's a fundamental need in life.

Golf is almost a religion for some people, and in fact, churches constituted the first clubs. People didn't find worshipping at home as fulfilling as doing it in the company of others, so they built churches. To this day, even if you do nothing but go to church, you fit the definition of club member because you sit in the pew to share your passion and common interest with like-minded people. That's what a club is about.

Clubs have been prevalent in America since it was founded. When early Americans settled the Great Plains, one of the major problems they encountered was the poor housewives practically going insane with boredom and loneliness, what with their husbands being out in the fields all day. It was no party for the men either—

the plow horse was not Mr. Ed. So farmers and ranchers formed grange societies that gave them venues for communing with others.

The club dynamic takes root early. Children, left to their own devices, form clubs with no provocation from adults, and the impulse never leaves them when they grow up. The engineer stuck in a high-rise building all week can feel a certain lack of human contact. He yearns to associate with people who like what he likes. So he joins the Shriners, the PTA, a chess club, an Internet chat room, or becomes a Red Cross volunteer. Maybe he joins the Hell's Angels. It doesn't matter. We all want to belong to something.

The person who enjoys golf and can afford to join a golf club is especially lucky. Golf clubs embody the best of our society and are a great symbol of the freedoms we enjoy. They are a tremendous asset to their cities and neighborhoods, and they contribute in ways no other clubs can. They are almost the equal of colleges or small universities.

The game their members play is self-governing, and they always play by the rules, on the course and off. The members abide by city and state laws and set high standards for local citizens. They generally are well-educated and insist that schools be the best quality possible. They own businesses that provide jobs. They pay taxes. The clubs are attractive and invariably the houses and developments near them are well-kept and maintain their real estate values.

Every week clubs are called upon to host all manner of civic and social functions, from business lunches to charity golf tournaments to weddings and bar mitzvahs to swimming meets. Their members know how to fund projects and organize events. Clubs provide jobs of every stripe.

Golf clubs are expected to serve our society, and they come through. They are underappreciated by our culture in general, and I dislike it when they are vilified out of misplaced perceptions or simple class envy. When Martha Burk attacked Augusta National Golf Club for not having women members, it angered me. In an interview for *Golf Digest*, I suggested that the next time Ms. Burk wanted to throw a wedding, maybe she'd phone a handball court— and send invitations to the thousand women who played Augusta the very year she attacked it. The best clubs are *not* exclusionary, and I had the sense she wanted to paint every club with the same brush. It just wasn't—and isn't—true.

The lure of rules and discipline

The revelations during the Enron investigation were astonishing. The executives who destroyed their company and ruined the lives of so many hardworking people were part of a circle—a club, if you will—that was chartered on greed and selfishness. The trouble with their "club" was that its members didn't know where the out-of-bounds stakes were. They viewed the rules as relative and tried to bend them in their favor. Can you imagine playing a twenty-dollar nassau against those guys?

People are attracted to clubs because they are places where rules and discipline thrive. Only in games do you have rules. When you open a box of checkers, the rules are right there on top. Individuals like a sense of order and fair play within a structured environment, and clubs offer those things in spades. Dress codes, etiquette, courtesy, and respect are the order of the day. They aren't merely appreciated, they're demanded.

New members tend to view the club's many rules as excessive—

at first. Over time they acquire an appreciation for them. A club's rules are similar to the rules that exist in the game itself in that they are expressed in black and white. A ball isn't halfway out-of-bounds; it's either in or it isn't.

The Enron criminals lived in a miserable world painted in varying shades of gray. They weren't interested in whether their activities were right or wrong; they only wanted to know if they were legal or illegal—and if the latter, how they could avoid getting caught.

The high cost of leisure

Golf has always been expensive, but I can't believe what it costs today. Green fees are too high and it costs too much to join a club. The expenses involved are tremendous and, in a lot of cases, unnecessary.

Take the courses we're building. Everybody wants to build the kind of golf courses they see on TV. They see these courses in their absolute peak condition and they want their course to be just like them. They want to feel—want to *say*—that the club they belong to is better than the one down the street. So they build courses that cost an absolute fortune. They don't just design eighteen holes, plant some grass, and build some greens. They move tons of dirt, and get a million people involved, from the government to engineers to the bulldozer operator to the environmentalists to the watering-system people.

Once the course is built, they have to run it, and that's expensive, too. There are a lot of hidden costs, things like labor costs, insurance, government taxes, property taxes. At Champions we have taxes on our guests who play. Just to register them, play golf, and have a drink, they are taxed. The deal is, if golf takes up a large piece of a community, the community says, "We're going to tax you because you have this privileged group here, and they make more money than we do and we need taxes for our school districts." Of course, nobody at the golf course goes to the school, but the poor golf course gets taxed out of existence because of the school district and God knows what else.

Choosing your members

It costs $25,000 to join Champions Golf Club. There are people who can afford a lot more than that, but that doesn't mean *we* can afford *them*. I'm talking about rich guys with high handicaps who primarily want to bring out guests, throw dinner parties, and show people how important they are. I prefer someone who can afford to get in, but who also has thousands of hours invested in the game. Say you paid a guy an hourly fee for the time he has put into golf. Add up those thousands of hours, and you'd owe that guy a lot of money. We get that guy and all he brings—his devotion, his adherence to the rules, his appreciation of tradition and competition—for that initiation fee. This is not the guy who cares more about a big dance floor than getting his clubs regripped. We get real golfers here, people who add to the fabric of this club. We go after the competitors.

I liken us to Stanford University, Yale, or Harvard. They don't accept D students academically, and we don't accept people with a D average in golf.

A healthy pack of bulldogs

Does my insistence on quality people make Champions elitist? It costs money to belong, but financial status notwithstanding, we make no exceptions either way for race, gender, religion, or anything else. I prefer that our members come from all walks of life, because if you put a hundred bulldogs inside a fenced yard and lock the gate, you'll one day wind up with some funny-looking bulldogs. A diverse membership adds vitality and breadth to a club.

I believe clubs in general have suffered because a few choose to be exclusionary. Although I strongly believe in a club's right to exclude people if it wishes—that's called the right of free association—it makes little sense to adopt exclusion as a routine policy. If you exclude women, for example, it causes a lot of discord within the family and the community. It siphons energy from the game.

Clubs that are inclusive can be harder to operate. They require more attention because they must offer more services—junior golf programs and ladies' day tournaments, for example. But these clubs amount to more as institutions. Clubs that exclude can never be beacons in their communities.

The assisted care facility

Many of the older clubs in the Northeast had hotels attached to the club, or at least a number of small apartments within their big, sprawling clubhouses. Westchester Country Club in New York is the best example, but Winged Foot and Metropolis had living quarters, too. Same thing with Brae Burn in Boston. In the South, Augusta National today has cabins on the property. At Champions we have a number of cottages along the course.

These clubs built housing for their older members. Rest homes were very rare in the old days, and when a club member became elderly, he often took up residence at the club. He had a place to eat and people to fraternize with. He could play gin rummy with his fellows or go down on the practice green and putt a little bit. There were always people nearby to look in on him. In a sense, the golf club was an assisted care facility. I believe in that ideal.

Older members are a great asset. They're the ones who help write the club histories. Invariably they have a kind word for everyone. They offer comfort and advice to the young people, tell the best stories, show the greatest interest in club competitions. They add immeasurably to the club's heritage and atmosphere.

These senior citizens may have had their day, but they are useful by their mere presence. When it's time for them to leave the treetops where they spent so many years, I don't want them breaking any branches on the way down.

Personally, I believe this applies to the staff as well. We have employees who have worked at Champions almost since its inception in 1957. It is not only their career, but a huge part of their lives. They understand our way of doing things. They know the members by name. They are as devoted to the club as the club is devoted to them. Even when they slow down a bit, that's okay. It's worth it. The loyalty we share is special.

When you visit really old Catholic churches and convents, you'll find many have burial grounds on the property. When the priests and nuns went to their reward, they were put in the ground right there. Not that I'd consider it, but if we offered burial plots at Champions, business would boom.

Youth must be served

On the other side of the spectrum you have the young people, and they too must be represented. For a club to thrive, or even survive, it must continually have an infusion of young players. I don't mean children, the sons and daughters of members already in place. Nor am I referring to clubs such as the Augusta Nationals of the world; they are a different animal entirely. I'm talking about the everyday club and course.

The young adults just out of college bring energy, spirit, and exuberance. They help maintain golf as a walking game instead of a riding game. The club is always new and exciting to them because they work for a living and cherish their visits to the course. Often they are the best players and always are well represented in club competitions.

Most clubs offer a junior class of membership to accommodate the young people, who haven't acquired enough wealth to pay the full freight. Clubs who do this are wise. The ones that do not aren't very smart, because you can't recruit new members from the graveyard.

Golf club or country club?

I have nothing against tennis, but I'd rather be shot in the leg than see tennis courts built at Champions. The reason I'm against tennis courts, swimming pools, lawn bowling, and the like is that they siphon attention away from golf. I want the club to have some semblance of balance, but in my world that means 90–10 in favor of golf.

Ancillary things like fitness centers, hairdressing salons, a big dance floor, and the like cost money to run. You always run the risk of them not pulling their weight. There are a few nights a year when we haul a portable dance floor out of storage, but I've tried not to make it too attractive. I almost hate to say it, but I fall in line with a middle-aged friend of mine who remarked, "The main reason I got married was so I wouldn't have to dance anymore."

We do host about twenty weddings a year and a few other outside events, but we charge handsomely for them. It can't be a break-even deal. If you're going to stage weddings, you might as well use the proceeds to defray the cost of golf.

Friend and foe

On one hand, the club manager is one of the club's greatest assets. He handles the employees, the dining room, outside events, holiday functions, and big club events such as the member-guest. He's in charge of the food and beverage service and much of the purchasing. His role is hugely important because it's oriented toward the bottom line. At many clubs he's viewed as more vital than the head pro.

The mere presence of the club manager is a challenge, because the business he operates falls almost entirely in the non-golf category. He wants it to thrive, and to do so he needs the budget weighted toward his end. Given a choice between new drapery and better drainage on three fairways, he'll vote for the drapes. He'll want to dress up the lunch menu. But he has to be reminded that people don't visit the club to buy cheeseburgers.

Running a club requires a good sense of balance. The president and board of directors need to be aware of where the pulls are coming from, and make their decisions wisely. They are in a difficult spot, because the club manager can create a lot of revenue. If the club manager stages ten more weddings than last year, it means the board members won't have to vote a dues increase for the membership—of which they are a part.

So the club basically needs to decide whether it wants to be an entertainment venue that provides decent golf on the side, or a thriving but affordable golf club that drums up business only as needed.

I prefer the latter. But that's just me.

The board member

Most boards consist of eccentric people. They customarily are powerful people who are used to imparting their will, think their way is the best way, and have a deep desire to leave their mark. Understand: They can't help themselves. Hang the *Mona Lisa* in a country club boardroom, and sooner or later an incoming president will lobby to have her hair repainted.

Sometimes the board member is caught in a crossfire between the club manager, his own better instincts, and his wife. When board members' wives are sending in the plays—like the club manager, they tend to vote for the drapes—you lose the type of balance I talked about earlier.

Taking the plunge

When Jimmy Demaret and I built Champions in 1957, I had no intention of building a swimming pool or tennis courts. We wanted it to be a golf club, not a country club. Then, in 1960, the fire marshal paid us a visit. Because Champions was in an area that at the time wasn't developed, we had no water resource in the event of a fire. The sprinkler system was inadequate. It would have cost a small fortune to run a line from some distant lake. After a bit of discussion, the fire marshal told us there was one solution we might want to consider.

Then and only then did we build a swimming pool. I confess I've never liked it. I've always tried to conceal it as best I can, but it's hard to miss because it's right outside my damned office. The wives and kids love it, though, so I accept that it's an imperfect world. And it's only open two months out of the year.

Flower power

People come to the club for relaxation and beauty. If you're going to be a beacon of the community, you want the place to stand out visually. If you belong to a club where nature does the planting, such as Shinnecock Hills or Cypress Point, good for you. But here in Texas, we don't have that sort of rugged beauty. We have to help it along. So we plant flowers, lots of them. Some people view flowers as an artificial affectation, but I disagree. We spend tens of thousands of dollars on flowers every year and have in our employ a full-time horticulturalist from England. Champions explodes with color almost all the time.

They pay to play

No question, golf club members are more affluent than the public at large. That creates a perception that the existing members paid for the beautiful clubhouse and golf course yesterday. Keep in mind though, that the club was paid for at its inception and in the middle years, and needs a perpetual flow of money to keep it going. If a club is fifty years old, can you imagine how much money the members have paid over the years? A lot of those people are no longer living, but the funds they injected into the club went a long way toward making it what it is today.

Clubs are perceived as rich, but as single entities they aren't wealthy at all. Their members may have money, but the clubs themselves are run as though they're nonprofit. Any revenue they generate goes right back into the club. Peter Drucker writes in his book *Managing for Results*, "Neither results nor resources exist inside the business. There are no profit centers within the business; there are only cost centers."

How deep are your roots?

The best restaurants, it seems to me, are ones that started out small with hopes of flourishing behind good food, excellent service, and a personal touch. If a great eatery excels at those things, it finds it can't accommodate all the people who want to eat there. When it turns a profit, the capital is used to expand. The larger version of the restaurant then succeeds on the same foundation—proven quality and service. Often you see a photograph of the original restaurant hanging on the wall of the new one.

The best clubs were established in a similar vein. A group of people would initially fund a club after determining that there were going to be enough members to make the plan feasible. Next would come a group of charter members, who put in additional money that took some of the pressure off the original investors. Then, before the course actually was finished, a drive for more members would be conducted. By the time the club was open, it would be well-grounded financially. That's because the founders never took their eyes off the ball.

Starting a club in a deliberate fashion makes sense not only from a fiscal standpoint, but also in terms of the identity, character, and future of the club. I think that the story of every club should start with, "In the beginning. . . ." For so many modern operations, there is no beginning. There is no evolution to speak of, no ripening of the atmosphere or gradual escalation into a grand institution.

Clubs today are created almost overnight. The swimming pool, tennis courts, and fitness center are there on opening day. The name of the club is almost an afterthought. If the designer told the developer the course would have a couple of pot bunkers, the developer will name it after something that's held a British Open.

One reason so many grandiose operations struggle or even fail is because they pour millions of dollars into creating the finished product, and then look around to see if the interest is there. I think it's wiser to start out small and grow based on overwhelming demand. It's dangerous to assume such a demand will exist based on the name of the architect or some misleading demographic study.

One of a kind

They say imitation is the sincerest form of flattery, but I'm not so sure. In the early 1990s, new clubs emerged in Arkansas, Kentucky, Florida, and Nebraska, each bearing the name "Champions." I was not amused. I sued to force these clubs to change their names, and won. It cost a ton of money, but to me it was worth it.

For thirty-five years, I'd strived to make Champions unique. If every course were named Champions, people would just go to the nearest one. We're not a supermarket chain. Just as only one horse can be named Secretariat, there can be only one Champions. When a person who graduated from the University of Notre Dame in Indiana—*the* Notre Dame—tells someone where he went to school, he is often asked, "Which one?" That's because there are a bunch of them.

Like I say, the court case was worth it. When Orville Moody tells someone he won the 1969 U.S. Open at Champions, they know which course he's talking about.

Race and golf

One of the more difficult moments for golf occurred in the summer of 1990, just prior to the PGA Championship at Shoal Creek in Birmingham, Alabama. Shoal Creek, like many clubs in America at that time, had no black members. When a reporter asked Hall Thompson, the club's chairman and founder, whether he intended to make his club more inclusive, Thompson said he had no intention of doing so. "The country club is our home and we pick and choose who we want," he was quoted as saying.

This was a national story. Protests were staged. Pressure was exerted on sponsors of the ABC telecast to withdraw their support. All of golf came under fire, as though clubs were joined in a large conspiracy to keep their institutions lily white.

On July 26, the producers of ABC's *Nightline* program phoned and asked if I would appear live on their telecast. I presumed they phoned me because at the time Champions had no African-American members. I agreed to appear along with the Reverend Abraham Woods, a Birmingham minister who rightfully was extremely upset by Hall Thompson's comments. The moderator for the discussion that evening was Chris Wallace, who did a very good job outlining the story and setting the table for our discussion.

Here are a few comments I made during the course of the conversation:

> *I'd love to have black members, but in the thirty-three years since Jimmy Demaret and I started this club, we've never had a black person fill out an application. We've had thousands of black people play our course. Black actors, ath-*

letes, and comedians have played here. But no one has applied for membership.

The only color we've ever discussed out here is the color green. We're not interested in people's color. We did not build Champions to exclude anyone on the basis of color. Anybody who wants to play golf and will abide by the rules of this club is welcome to come here. We can't go out and lasso people off the streets and try to get them in here. We can't go after Iraqis, Russians, and whomever you want to name. Any black person in the city of Houston who wants to play can fill out an application. The minutes of our meetings will show that we do not discriminate against anyone.

It is not the policy of a golf club to recruit anyone. We don't recruit whites. That's the policy of a football team. Our feeling is, if you can play, bring it on.

I think that people who practice exclusionary policies are very insecure people. I don't believe in building an exclusive athletic facility that excludes anyone. But I'm not going to go out on the streets of Houston and ask anyone to join.

We have blacks who play here almost every day, have lunch at Champions every day. I have been amazed that not one man has ever come over here and asked to be a member of this club. Look, we'd like more people to support this facility. In Texas, with the [economic] condition we've been in, getting new members is the name of the game. These are very expensive facilities here. If you have a modern-day club with these big clubhouses, you better have some open arms.

Our club is open, it always has been, and always will be.

I've competed all my life in this golf game and I've never excluded anyone. We're going to play by the rules, and we're going to run this club by the rules. And that means we will exclude no one.

As the interview wound down, Wallace asked about the Masters and Augusta National Golf Club, which at the time had no black members, either. I pointed out that Augusta National had a very small membership, but that its members also happened to be some of the most prominent CEOs in America. I said that if more minorities happened to acquire those CEO positions, they might be asked to join a club like Augusta. "You have to be asked to join," I said. "You just don't drive up to the gates and ask to be let in."

Not long after that interview, a man named Walter King submitted an application at Champions and became our first black member. The numbers have increased here, as at clubs elsewhere across America. Some very positive strides were made socially in the wake of the Shoal Creek controversy.

We didn't seek Walter out. I still believe clubs shouldn't feel obliged to run out and get one of everybody—one Irishman, one Scot, one black, one Italian, one Iraqi, one Jewish fellow, whatever. Around the time of the *Nightline* interview, I read somewhere that eleven percent of the population of this country is Russian or of Russian descent. So where does it stop? I don't think clubs should be run like Noah's Ark. They should run unencumbered by all of these things.

I was complimented for appearing on *Nightline* when representatives from the PGA of America, the PGA Tour, and other high-profile entities refused to come on. They may have been afraid of saying the wrong thing in the wrong way at the wrong time. But I wasn't the least bit nervous discussing the situation. I was raised in a caddie yard, like most golfers were seventy years ago, and there were only one or two white kids in the caddie yard out of maybe a hundred caddies. I was raised around the problems of minorities. In fact, I couldn't get into the clubhouse myself. I was raised pretty much "not being able to get in." Hell, even pros had trouble getting into the clubhouse back then. So I understand a little bit about where blacks and other minorities are coming from.

A lot of the discrimination in this country is economic. Companies put a lot of white people into country clubs, either directly or through the money they pay them that enables them to afford it. As soon as we start seeing more blacks with prominent positions in industry, we'll see more blacks in clubs.

Kind words for George

When there's a problem with an employee, I want that employee whipped into shape. We lean hard on our department heads to get that done. The workers have a responsibility to us. They are family, and to some degree we have a responsibility to them. I don't want them to leave.

We had an employee named George who worked in the locker room. George passed away a few years ago, so I'm comfortable telling this story about him. One day I called him into my office.

"George, I have some good news for you," I said. "I want to tell you to your face that you will never be fired from this job."

"Thank you, Mr. Burke," he said. "What did I do?"

"George, you're staying because you're so bad that you make the rest of us look great. I'd like to remind you that the soap belongs in the soap dish and not on the floor of the shower, and that it probably wouldn't break your back to pick up the towel that a member leaves by his locker."

George was hugely embarrassed. He very nearly started crying. I got up from my chair, walked around the desk, and put my hand on his shoulder. I said, "I'm just trying to make something out of you, George, and I'm not going to let you let me down. Now get back to work."

I never had a better employee than George after that.

Please, borrow our credo

The club has to work hard for its members and its guests. The effort has to be unrelenting. Champions is a large club and we have many visitors from across the U.S. and worldwide. Their stay here has to be special. They must leave with a fresh, positive imprint of what we are about.

We have a saying: "Every Day Is Opening Day." It's the only credo we live by. That's a big challenge in an era when you hear people talk about getting "burned out," but it can be done if you've got the right mind-set.

The secret is enthusiasm. Life is about reinventing yourself and your attitude toward work every day. As a player, I tried to perform at a high level, albeit a little differently, every time I got out of bed. If you have the mental flexibility to do that, you're way ahead of the game, whether it's golf or anything else.

CHAPTER FIVE

Just Go Play

Hints to help you score better

As an assistant pro at Winged Foot in 1949, I got to know another assistant named George Schoux. The club had a large stable of assistants at the time—all of us young, ambitious, and serious about our games. But George took these traits to a higher level. Realizing there was no better golf course in the world for developing a quality game than Winged Foot, George played and practiced like the devil.

He didn't just play eighteen holes in the afternoon after work and then practice until dark. We all did that. George would work on his game into the middle of the night. Winged Foot members frequently told of leaving the club at 2 A.M. after a long night of playing cards and finding George putting on the practice green, flashlights illuminating the holes.

To keep him company, George kept a small doll in his back pocket. He nicknamed the doll Virgil. After holing a difficult putt, George would whip the doll out of his pocket and say, "What did you think of that one, Virgil?" That doll went everywhere with him. When George turned his back, you could see Virgil from the chest

Birdieing the last three holes to win happens by accident. It isn't in the plans. To finish strong, you must think only of executing each shot as it comes.

•

The place to find your swing is on the golf course, not the practice range.

up. George was a strange dude. But he could putt like a dream, and Hogan never hit it better.

When the day came that George thought his game was ready, he left Winged Foot to try the pro tour. When word got back to the club a couple of weeks later that George won the first tournament he played in, the Richmond Open out in California, we weren't a bit surprised. I'm telling you, George could flat-out play.

As good a player as George was, I secretly wondered how much of his ability was attributable to his obsessive practice. I know it helped him some, but I suspected his success was more a result of natural talent. For George, practice seemed to be an end in itself.

Golf is a powerful stimulant. There is an addictive quality to it that causes some people to develop a mindless approach. Their behavior is similar to that of joggers who force themselves to run five miles every day even if they're sick. We all know "range rats," golfers who are on the range daily, bashing balls for long periods of time. They have a vague notion that just being on the range whacking balls will somehow do their game a world of good. Usually nothing constructive seeps through, because they lose their awareness of what they need to do to get better.

Improving at golf requires constant attention to visualization, timing, balance, feel, and touch. It demands an open mind to the secrets of shooting your best score, not just obsessive attention to your golf swing. It's easy to lose sight of that when you beat 200 balls on the range or get in a cart and fly around the course as fast as you can.

I didn't quite finish the story about George Schoux. After his victory in Richmond, he never won again and sort of drifted away. Eventually he wound up in a mental hospital. Whether it was his obsession with practicing all the time that put him there, or if that was just a symptom of something deeper, I'm not qualified to say. But all that practice didn't help.

Trust and faith

When I was growing up, my dad insisted that we be at Mass at 7 A.M. every Sunday morning. No matter how late we were up the night before, we were expected to be at St. Anne's church—and in the front row. My father was a man of tremendous faith. He trusted God and he trusted himself—you don't finish second in the U.S. Open without having trust in your swing.

Faith and trust are important in golf. Faith especially is one of the essences of the game. If all we get out of it is what we've gotten so far, we'd find something else to do. We have to have faith that there are better things in store, that we'll improve and have greater success.

As for trust, there are golfers who don't have the same trust in themselves that they have in others in everyday life. They have plenty of skill, yet seem to play poorly in competition. We state the obvious about a player when we say, "He isn't a good competitor" or, "He's not good under pressure," but what we're saying is that he doesn't trust his swing or his courage to make his best putting stroke when it counts.

The best way to create trust is to be a realist. If you can accept that you'll fail once in a while, it will help you relax and trust what you're doing. It seems like twice a year I see a major-league pitcher accidentally throw a ball over the screen behind home plate, or watch a top golfer hit a shank on national television. But they are smart enough to know that their comical failing was a fluke and is unlikely to happen again very soon.

Escaping the comfort zone

Golfers have a hard time dealing with success. It's very difficult for the average 10-handicapper to shoot even par on the front nine and keep the momentum going on the back nine. A certain fear sets in, a feeling that he isn't good enough to have done what he did. He almost feels relieved when he double-bogeys the tenth hole.

When I won the four tournaments in a row in 1952, I had an incredible feel with the putter given to me by Otey Crisman. After the second win, I could feel a little doubt trying to creep into my mind that this just could not keep up. At the same time, I knew that if I accepted that thought, I would stop playing well. The thought of placing a cap on my potential made me angry.

I'm not sure why the mind tells you that you have enough success and to back off. But you have to train yourself to ignore it. The first step is to recognize that the thought is natural and to understand that it will steal something from you.

Then you come up with any mental technique you can to fight it off. Sometimes you fight it through sheer force of will. In my case, I felt that my clubs didn't know that I was winning and my putter had no idea it was rolling a lot of long putts into the hole. I knew these things had no bearing at all on the next shot I was about to hit.

What matters most

The game of golf comes down to making the clubface arrive at the ball in a square position, and travel with the right amount of speed.

Imagine what we've gone through trying to master that simple act! But it's a fundamental you should keep in mind. I learned that from an episode at Winged Foot during my assistant pro days in 1949.

There were a lot of one-day tournaments for local pros in those days, and we assistants played in them whenever Claude Harmon, the head pro, saw fit to give us the day off. These tournaments were important to us because they kept our games sharp competitively and, even more important, gave us the opportunity to win some money. Whatever we won, we'd divide equally among ourselves.

There was one event at Piping Rock, out on Long Island, that was an exceptionally good one. It was conducted partly to raise money for charity, and was a pro-am competition. There were four divisions—individual, with an adult as a partner, with a child as a partner, and with a lady as a partner.

I wasn't playing well leading up to the event, and Claude refused to give me permission to play. "You're hitting the ball all over the lot and I think it would be just a waste of time," he said. Somehow I persuaded Claude to let me go down anyway. That night, lying in bed, I strained to think of a way to keep the ball on the golf course. Finally, I boiled it down to the basics. I decided I would take the club back a certain way and at all costs bring the club into the ball the same way it was at address, in that perfectly square position. I decided not to watch the ball after it left the clubface until it practically hit the ground. The rest I would leave to chance.

I went out to Piping Rock the next day and shot 70. I won every way possible. Back at Winged Foot, I laid a check for $1,800 in the middle of the table and couldn't wait to get Claude's reaction. He looked at the check, then at me, then back at the check.

"I think you got lucky," he said, and sauntered out of the room.

Always have a target. If
you aim at nothing, you'll
hit it every time.

•

Play match play as though
it were medal play.

Leave it to Claude to bring a guy back down to earth. But I'd already taken with me an important lesson about having the clubface square at impact.

Bing's work ethic

Bing Crosby enjoyed coming to Champions to play golf for a few days and relax. Sometimes he brought along his sons Nathaniel and Harry. Nathaniel developed into a fine player and won the U.S. Amateur at the Olympic Club in San Francisco. I'm his godfather.

There was one visit where Bing didn't play much. He was preparing for a big performance in Houston that included a Mexican tune he really wanted to sing. But he was having a terrible time getting the inflection of a certain phrase just right. He rehearsed the song constantly in the main dining room, to no avail. Finally Bing looked up a well-known Mexican girl singer in town and had her come out to Champions. She knew the Mexican song by heart and Bing had her sing it over and over again. Then Bing sang it several more times until he had it just right.

Once Bing had the song down, he did play a little golf with Nathaniel and Harry. But from that visit I discovered two principles behind his success that happen to apply to golf. The first is, little things count. Bing could have muddled his way through that one phrase in Spanish, but that wasn't good enough for him. In golf, you should never neglect practicing the little things, like when your ball is up against the fringe near the green, or your short putting, or from bad lies.

Second, although Bing was immensely talented, you can bet he put in a great deal of time honing his craft. Natural talent goes a long way, but it won't take you *all* the way unless you work harder than the next person.

The sound of music

One of my favorite golf partners was Sugar Ray Robinson, the great middleweight boxing champion. Sugar Ray wasn't an outstanding golfer, but I always came away from a round with him swinging more smoothly than usual. It wasn't his swing; it was the way he walked. He glided around the course with a tempo and ease of movement that was contagious.

Sam Snead had the same quality, an inner syncopation that was never rushed and never broken. Ernie Els has it, Julius Boros had it, and my friend Steve Elkington has it. You either have that quality or you don't. But if you seek out someone with a "natural" swing and play with him a lot, some of it might rub off on you.

A bargain at any price

Harvey Penick had a saying: "Go to dinner with good putters." He felt that the positive attitude shared by skilled putters was contagious. Conversely, hanging around sour people who complain about bad breaks will infect your outlook. Harvey possessed a lot of wisdom, a lot of it coming out of the evenings he spent at the Burke dinner table back in the 1930s.

I would expand on Harvey's comment to say you should play with players who are better than you are. Play for a few dollars; the education will be well worth the cost. Nothing will put fire in your belly like getting your butt beat. Lose a few dollars and you *will* find a way to get the ball in the hole faster.

Think through your hands,
not your muscles.

•

The serious competitor is
often viewed as a hard
case, a person who is
tough to get along with.
Give him some leeway—the
only alternative is
to not try at all. He's
choosing the better
of two evils.

The St. Petersburg compact

In 1952, on the Monday after I'd won three PGA Tour events in a row, I was feeling so good (and so tired) that I decided not to drive from Louisiana to the next tournament in St. Petersburg, Florida. I elected to fly instead. Tommy Bolt came with me, and we left it to our caddies to drive our cars ahead to Florida. We got to St. Petersburg all right, but the caddies did not. They happened to be black, and while we were waiting for our clubs, I got a call from the sheriff in a small town saying it didn't look right—two black fellows driving Cadillacs through his county at 2 A.M. He'd hauled them in. By the time we got our caddies released and they made it to St. Pete, it was late Wednesday and I was like a caged cat, nervous about going more than two days without practicing. I teed off on Thursday after hitting just a few balls that morning.

It turned out to be a blessing. At that point in my career, I wasn't too sure of myself, and I'd gone from feeling tremendously confident to very worried. By winning at St. Petersburg, I learned that being a little worried is a great asset. When you're on edge, you're alert and perceptive. On the other side, confidence can kill you. How many times have you played a terrific round on Saturday, had the feel of an angel, and assumed that on Sunday you'd merely pick up where you left off—and then played terribly? When you're that confident, the shock of "not having it" can make it impossible to ever get going. It's one of the things golfers learn as they go along, making them say the things they do about golf being a humbling game.

After St. Petersburg, I made a covenant with myself to stay on edge, to be mindful that yesterday was a million years ago. We've all had days when we make every putt we look at, when we drive the ball a mile with no effort, and our irons go right at the flag. The next day nothing goes right because we assumed there would be more miracles rather than paying attention to business. In this game, it's very foolish to try to bring yesterday forward.

Targets in the sky

When the wind is blowing, your target is the wind itself. Imagine the ball at the peak of its trajectory and what the wind will do to it from there. That's the moment when wind really takes hold of the ball—just as it begins to lose energy at the peak of its flight. If you see the wind blowing your ball fifteen feet to the left, aim at a window in the sky fifteen feet to the right of your objective.

How to choose the right club, every time

Stomping around in search of a sprinkler head that has "162" stamped on it is a complete waste of time. Before they invented the 150-yard marker, Ben Hogan, Sam Snead, and the rest of us used a formula that worked better than numbers. Look toward the green and determine what club you'd need to use—with $1,000 riding on it—to fly the ball to the very back of the green. You have to be honest with yourself; there's $1,000 at stake, so you better not underclub. If that club is a 6-iron, simply take one club less—the 7-iron—and hit it firmly or softly depending on whether the hole is front, middle, or back. This formula never fails. It also teaches you feel, touch, and a sense for wind and the elevation of the green. One more thing: It will cut half an hour off your round.

Sometimes we win
because we control our
performance and expect
success. Most of the time,
though, we win because
others lose. Be cautious
about judging yourself a
"champion."

•

Use the terrain to your
advantage. If you don't
control the land,
it will control you.

Let's be reasonable

I very rarely aimed at the flagstick, because unless I bounced my ball off it, I had failed. I always wanted to feel like I had succeeded. Why aim at something I couldn't hit with a rifle?

Broaden your target. Your confidence will grow, you'll relax, and you'll play better.

Walls of aluminum

Sometimes you can score well despite a part of your game not being in top shape. Such was the case with me at the 1955 Rubber City Open. I was driving the ball terribly, but chipped, putted, and recovered so well that I found myself in a four-man playoff. I knew that to have any chance of winning, I had to find a way to put the ball in the fairway. While sipping a cool drink before the playoff, I closed my eyes and imagined the fairway of the first playoff hole being lined with tall, solid walls made of Alcoa aluminum. My intent was to free up my swing and not care where the ball went—after all, if I pushed or pulled my drive, the aluminum "walls" would deflect the ball back into the fairway.

I proceeded to make one of the best swings of my life and split the middle of the fairway. I didn't win the playoff; Henry Ransom chipped in to beat me and the others. But I left town feeling pretty good about myself. I'd discovered the importance of freeing up the swing under pressure, and found a bit of mental imagery that helped me do it.

When you're choking

When the pressure is getting to you and you feel like your game is about to fall apart, the only thing to do is to swing as hard as you can with every club and hope you make contact with the ball. Don't worry where the ball will go. Just hit it, find it, and hit it again. Swinging all-out—and by that I mean making a big turn while keeping your muscles loose—often helps you find your timing.

"Little Runny"'s secret

Paul Runyan won the PGA Championship in 1934 and 1938, and in those years was always at or near the top of the money list. Into the late 1950s and early 1960s, he was among the best senior players in the nation. Looking at Paul, it was almost hard to believe he had these credentials. He stood only about five-foot-seven, and weighed 130 pounds soaking wet. He could carry the ball only 210 yards with his driver.

Paul had to squeeze every yard possible out of his slight frame. I asked him once about his swing philosophy—he was a thoughtful man and one of the best teachers of all time—and he gave me an interesting answer. "I'm very concerned going back and I don't give a damn coming down," was his reply. Paul felt, as I do, that the backswing should be performed with care and caution, while the forward swing should be reckless.

A tall order

If you find yourself trying extra hard on a shot you deem especially important, you're selling yourself short. It's as though you put no effort into executing the shots that came before it. You definitely want to pay close attention to a critical shot, but don't change the amount of time you spend executing it. That's a tall order, but the best players are able to do that. Tiger Woods spends no more time on a putt to win a tournament than he does on a putt on the first green. It's true; he's been timed with a stopwatch and there's virtually no change.

When you place too much emphasis on a single stroke (usually one late in the round), it usually comes off poorly. Taking extra time is the big culprit because you give tension time to set in. The next thing you know you're staring down at the ball thinking only of making perfect contact. You have to find the courage to let the shots flow out of your body.

What I learned from Tiger

During one of the Tour Championships at Champions a few years ago, I congratulated Tiger Woods on how well he was handling the media. At the time there was no instance of him saying anything inflammatory or something that offended the PGA Tour or his fellow players. Come to think of it, his record is unblemished to this day.

Tiger thanked me for the compliment. Then he added, "My dad taught me that when I'm asked a question, I have control of the answer."

That's a simple realization and it applies to the way we play the game, too. Every time a question is presented to you on the golf course—a 185-yard shot over water from a bad lie, for example—you have control of the answer. You can either lay up or go for it, depending on your patience, trust, and ability to actually pull the shot off. Unless you are desperate, you shouldn't take an unnecessary chance unless you have an eighty-five percent chance of pulling it off. A little caution means less stress and tension, and a better chance of making a good swing.

When you walk to your
ball between shots, keep
your head up. Look
around and be observant.
In the jungle, animals who
keep their heads down
get eaten.

•

The best instruction books
are helpful enough.
But you'll learn more
by watching than by
reading.

Give it a rest

My dad used to tell me that the person who was well-rested had a big edge. He believed in getting a good night's sleep before a competitive round. But I took Dad's advice a step further. I found a way to rest during the round.

A round of golf lasts four hours or more. I couldn't concentrate intensely for that long, because it took too much out of me. So I didn't concentrate furiously on every hole. When I came to a par 3 with a ridiculously hard hole location, I would relax and hit a standard shot to the middle of the green. I would save my grinding for the putt.

I did the same thing on a par 5 I couldn't reach in two. I'd hit my drive smoothly, not putting too much pressure on myself to hit it very far or especially straight. Walking down the fairway to play my second shot, I'd let my mind wander a bit. I'd relax on the second shot, too, not being sloppy but merely advancing it into position to play my third. The third shot I'd bear down on. And of course I'd try my best on the putt. But by taking half the hole "off" mentally, I conserved a lot of energy.

One for the ladies—and some of the guys

I read these days about men getting in touch with their feminine sides, but I'd like to see more women get in touch with their masculine sides. It is very difficult to get most women to swing violently enough. They are inclined to be dainty, and golf is not at all a dainty game.

This generalization doesn't apply to women who took up the game at a young age or who played other sports growing up. But many women don't take up the game until they are in their thirties or forties, when they have more time to devote to it. It's harder to instill a sense of recklessness in a person who hasn't played other sports extensively.

For what it's worth, there are men who need to go at the ball more aggressively, too. As a teacher, I'd rather take on a beginner who is too violent and try to scale him or her back, than the other way around.

Can you see the game?

I asked a good pool player once if he played the game one shot at a time. "I don't see shots," he said. "I see the game." He explained that he saw the pool table and balls in a large, general way. His mind would digest the image very quickly and within a few seconds he could see several shots being played in correct sequence.

Some golfers "see" the game faster than others. Jimmy Demaret and Ben Hogan were nearly the same age, but Jimmy developed faster than Ben (and played a lot faster) because he could glance at a hole and immediately see the proper way to play it. Ben had to study a hole longer before deciding which strategy was best. In later years he talked about course management and strategy a lot because they didn't come easily for him.

How quickly you see the game doesn't necessarily determine how well you play, but it does determine how fast you play. If you labor over what type of shot to play and where to place it, you weren't blessed with that gift. Only experience will endow you with it.

Don't call in sick

The true competitor plays even when he's tired or not feeling well. Golf is one sport where this is possible, because although you're

Don't let the thought of improving turn into a fantasy. We have enough dreamers. Get out on the course and go to work.

•

To get used to winning, you first have to do a lot of losing.

expending energy, it comes out of you gradually. Try to tough it out. Your clubs don't know you have a fever. Sometimes you'll actually play better, because you're so preoccupied with feeling bad that you play as if you're on automatic pilot. You don't have enough strength to overswing.

Low beats high

I attended a clinic once in which three amateurs hit shots for the audience, after which the instructor made some remarks about each player. There was a poor player, an average player, and a top-flight player, who happened to be a teenager. The youngster was something, striping every shot. When the clinic was finished, I approached the boy's father and asked him how he taught his son to hit the ball so solidly. He told me he hammered two stakes into the ground and strung a rope between them so it was three feet off the ground. He then positioned his son ten feet from the rope and had him hit 7-iron shots with the directive that each shot fly under the rope.

Hitting the ball low like that takes some doing. Your hands must lead the clubhead and you must shift your weight to the left. What a terrific exercise that is for any golfer. Low beats high in almost every game, and it's certainly the way to go in golf. The wind doesn't affect the ball as much. You tend to hit the ball more crisply. You can fly the ball to the target or bounce it in there. You have more control.

The best low-ball hitters *don't* play the ball back in their stance. Your ball position for the irons never changes. I asked Ben Hogan once why he never moved the ball around in his stance, and he replied, "I'm not good or smart enough to do that." Ben played all his iron shots with the ball a few inches to the right of his left heel, and adjusted his ball flight by varying how far ahead of the ball his hands were at address and through impact. When Ben's hands were low on his follow-through, you knew he was trying to keep the ball down.

Hogan the chameleon

At the Phoenix Open one year, I shot 68 in the first round and was eager to get back to the hotel. I was playing well and no part of my game needed a great deal of work. As I walked past the practice range on the way to the parking lot, I saw Ben Hogan there hitting balls. Ben had won the previous week, which piqued my curiosity. What could he possibly be working on? I made a detour to the range, said hello to Ben, and sat on his bag to watch.

Ben was practicing with his right thumb and forefinger off the shaft. It was hard to detect because they were very near the shaft, but they clearly weren't touching the club. I'd tried this and knew that it made it easier to waggle the club and break your wrists earlier in the swing. Ben had a driver in his hands and he was hitting every shot just perfect. I watched Ben for a while, hit some balls myself, then made it back to the hotel.

The next day Ben shot 69. I saw him after the round and asked him about taking the thumb and index finger off the shaft. I was curious if he had actually played that way.

"Oh, that," he said. "That one never made it to the first tee."

Ben experimented a lot. He tried things all the time, sometimes keeping a small technique for months, sometimes for a day, other times for five minutes. He made minor changes constantly, sometimes in the middle of a round.

Experiment with your swing. It's fun, stimulating, and educational. Golf is a form of recreation, a word rooted in "re-create." It's a wonderful way to learn, and over time you'll find a lot of keys that will help you play better.

Jimmy's way

Jimmy Demaret's playing technique was shaped by his hard times coming up. He grew up desperately poor, and talked about his family living on "highway stew"—freshly killed animals struck by automobiles near his home in Houston. Jimmy came to River Oaks looking for work by wading barefoot across a bayou to get there. His father had died, and my father took him under his wing, becoming a kind of foster dad to him. Jimmy actually baby-sat me when I was very small, and as I grew older he became like a brother to me.

When Jimmy grew up and decided to try the pro tour, he found out the purses were too small for him to make a decent living. In order to make enough money to eat, Jimmy decided to eliminate one side of the golf course. He hook-proofed his swing by weakening his left-hand grip and refusing to let the clubface close through impact. He rolled his wrists, which gave him plenty of power, but at the same time he bowed the back of his left wrist to stop the club from closing excessively. He succeeded in eliminating the left side of every golf course he played, hitting a beautiful, powerful fade. His control was so good that he won the Masters three times, even though Augusta National favored a draw. In my estimation he was one of the greatest, most influential players who ever lived. I always thought Ben Hogan learned something about hitting a fade from watching Jimmy.

I didn't have the strength in my hands that Jimmy did, so it was hard for me to adopt his playing style. It would be hard for just about anybody, especially the everyday golfer. But I did adopt a similar technique with the putter. I found that by weakening my left-hand grip—rotating my left hand counterclockwise so the back of the hand faced the target—I couldn't miss a putt to the left. That helped my putting immensely. I might misread a putt or push it to the right, but I rarely pulled a putt to the left.

When you go to the practice green, try developing a stroke that makes it difficult to miss on one side or the other. It's easier to putt knowing you can only miss one way.

Playing from sand

When playing from a greenside bunker, try to throw the sand as high in the air as possible. This will help you take the right amount of sand (hit about four inches behind the ball), which is the key to getting the ball close to the hole.

Say hello to "George"

Set up for the sand shot as though the flagstick were a person named George, and you were going to speak to him. That means you align your body to the left of the flagstick, not so you are facing George directly, but at a slight angle.

When you play the shot, throw the sand just to the left of George. Remember to unwind your hips and shoulders fully, as on any other shot. How fast you unwind them depends on the length of the shot—the longer the shot, the fuller and faster the motion.

Perfect pitches

The twenty-yard pitch gives a lot of players fits, which is ironic because the swing is so small. The trouble is that there's so little mar-

The outcome of a shot,
regardless of the distance,
is largely determined by
the pace of your
backswing.

•

Learn to play the par 3s
well. Scores of "2" don't
add up very fast.

gin for error. If you hit the ball a bit fat, the clubhead doesn't have enough speed to pass through the ball. If you hit the ball thin—well, let's say you have more than enough speed.

The key is how you use your hands—or don't use them. You need to break your wrists on the backswing and then keep them cocked on the downswing. If you uncock your wrists, you are done—you'll hit the ball fat or thin every time. To get the club back to the ball, you simply turn through the ball using your knees, hips, and shoulders. Let your arms lag behind your upper body and keep your wrists cocked.

This technique works from greenside bunkers, too.

CHAPTER SIX

Good-bye Ain't Always Gone

Reflections on my favorite people

I've described my early adult years as being lean financially, but my life didn't start out that way. My family was very well off. My father was the first golf pro in Texas and his services were much in demand. When he was head pro at River Oaks Country Club in Houston, his salary was $30,000 per year. In the 1920s and especially during the Great Depression, that was a huge amount of money. A lot of the River Oaks members were oil people who could afford to pay him well. We had a big house, a nice car, a cook, and a maid. Our family didn't live extravagantly, but we had few of the worries other families did.

Solvent though we were, it still was an era when golf professionals weren't fully accepted socially. My father rarely went into the clubhouse; at that time, pros weren't permitted there. His children, me included, weren't allowed to hang around the pro shop. I spent my days in the caddie yard with the other caddies, most of whom were black and underprivileged. The yard would be filled with as many as a hundred kids hoping to have their names called so they could make a little money. On a good day at River Oaks, perhaps eighty players would tee off, so there were lot of days when not all the caddies "got a bag."

The caddie yard was a rough place. We chipped, putted, shot dice, and gambled on anything. Gambling is part of life to many Texans; it goes on constantly to this day. I think gambling was in the blood of the settlers who came here. It was a huge risk moving to Texas in the first place, trying to scratch out a living in a harsh climate on pretty unforgiving land. Because the area wasn't well-populated, there wasn't much to do socially. So gambling became an everyday form of stimulation.

I learned a little about golf and a lot about survival in that caddie yard. The fact I was the son of the pro didn't sit well with some of the other caddies. One day one of them remarked, "If you weren't the son of the pro, I'd kick your ass."

"If I were you, I'd start right now," I said. Taking this kid on then and there wasn't possible because we'd both get suspended from the yard for good. So we arranged to meet at the course at six the following morning and have it out. When we arrived the next day, we were the only ones there. We started fighting and went at it until we both were exhausted, then took a rest. When we got our wind back, we fought some more until we got tired again. We kept fighting, on and off, until 9 A.M. Finally, we called it off. It was a draw, and he never bothered me again. I don't think I even told Mom or Dad about it.

The expression you always heard around the caddie pen was "It's hard in the yard." It was that for sure. When the kids who did get out to caddie came back to the yard after the round, the others were waiting for them, dice or cards in hand, to try to take their money. They'd sharpened their swords all day. It was pretty cut-throat.

I came out of the caddie yard with a good feeling toward caddies that has prevailed my entire life. For most of them, there was very little possibility of rising up and getting a good education or establishing a good career. I felt a great deal of empathy for them, especially the ones who showed ability as golfers. There were a lot of talented kids who never had the means or opportunity to succeed as I did.

Caddies are my favorite people in golf. They are a source of comedy, golf psychology, wisdom, and encouragement. Caddies young and old are part of the fabric of any good golf club. Sadly, they are slowly drifting away from the game, replaced by carts and shunned by clubs and resort courses that are apathetic about the contributions they make.

How "Pappy" handled a champion

Warm as I felt toward caddies, as a pro I never was comfortable relying on their input. When I was assigned a caddie at the beginning of a tournament week, I would issue the same speech: "If you will stand two club lengths from my ball at all times, and don't step onto the putting green once, you will get a very nice tip when we're finished."

I broke this policy only one time. After playing a bunker shot to four feet on the eighteenth hole at the 1956 Masters, I surveyed the putt and didn't like what I saw one bit. It was downhill, slightly left to right and fast as the devil. This putt was so frightening, the consequences of missing it so great, I felt like I was going to pass out. That's when I called Pappy over.

Pappy—I never knew his real name—was one of the great Augusta National caddies. He had carried the bags of three other champions before me, and knew every dip and swale on that golf course. Pappy always carried one of my clubs in his left hand as he walked, twirling it casually. It was comforting watching him, as though he were transferring mystical energy into my clubs. I'd never relied on Pappy to do anything much, but I needed him now.

"It's inside the left edge, right?" I whispered to him.

Pappy took a look at the putt, placed his hand on my shoulder, and said in a soothing voice, "It sure is, pro. Just go on and cruise her on in there."

I made the putt—I don't know how I did it—and have always felt grateful to Pappy for that small confirmation of my read. Regardless of how that putt broke, he wasn't about to dispute my notion that it was left edge all the way. Pappy knew that disputing my opinion would only confuse me and make a difficult putt that much harder.

Pappy's gone, but when I get to the big clubhouse in the sky, I'm going to thank him again for handling me just right.

Let's give it up

When you're playing as a guest, offer to pay for your caddie. And don't ask your host how much you should pay him. Be generous. Think of what you paid a caddie the last time you used one, and give him twenty dollars over that amount. For God's sake, help the guy out. I've never seen a caddie leave the parking lot in a Cadillac.

Body language

When I played the tour, caddies frequently got into tight spots, money-wise. What money they made was often lost gambling, drinking, or carrying on in some other fashion. They often turned to players for a "loan," which, often as not, was forgotten.

I got used to them asking for money. When I saw a caddie approaching me and he had his palms up, I knew he was going to ask for a loan. They were just like television evangelists—when they ask for charity, they always have their palms up. I would say, "If we're going to talk, we're going to do it with our palms down." That was surprisingly difficult for them to do. In explaining the reason for needing a few dollars, at some point their palms would go up again. Check for yourself—when somebody wants something from you, their hands are in front of them, palms up.

The modern caddie

Tour players all have regular caddies now. It's interesting how the player and caddie are almost like a small company. The business arrangements between them are growing more complex. Insurance, travel, and salary are all agreed upon in advance. It may not be long before the player starts a human resources department just for the man carrying his bag.

The caddie is almost like a celebrity. When "Fluff" Cowan worked for Tiger Woods, he even made a television commercial. And they make a very good living; they should have a money list for caddies. The best ones make more than any club pro in the nation.

The ne'er-do-well

Most caddies these days are young kids, teenagers, or college students, and that's fine. But I miss the adult caddies. A few still exist today, full-time loopers who work the summers up north and winters in Florida. They are readily identifiable. Most are fiercely independent, proud of their calling, divorced, like to drink beer, enjoy the racetrack, and are dead honest.

A free lesson

People are highly imitative, and in my era it certainly held true for the way caddies moved from one shot to the next. The bag would be slung over the right shoulder and in the left hand they held one of your clubs. As they moseyed along the fairway, they would idly swat at pine cones and loose pieces of turf.

What I noticed was the caddies always had a perfect left-hand grip, the handle pressed against the palm with the fingers, the thumb placed closely alongside the index finger. Some played golf in their spare time, others did not. But they always held the club correctly. Pappy was like that.

If you're a beginning golfer or an inexperienced one, practice holding and swinging a club with your left hand only. Chances are, you'll instinctively hold it correctly.

High living

A caddie I knew told me of seeing his minister wearing a lot of gold around his neck. Alarmed by this ostentatious display of wealth, he confronted him.

"Preacher, isn't that a lot of gold for a humble servant of the Lord to be wearing?" he asked.

The minister said, "If you are a good man in this world, you will one day go to heaven and walk the Golden Road. All the gold around my neck means is I'm just getting the feel of it before I get there."

Until next time

My favorite caddie was a fellow at Winged Foot known to everyone as "Wingie." Over the years I saw a lot of Wingie, not only in the New York area, but around Miami, where he'd migrate each winter.

When I'd leave town for a tournament, I'd always find Wingie to wish him well and tell him good-bye. His answer, given with a happy smile, was always the same. "Good-bye ain't always gone."

CHAPTER SEVEN

SOME THOUGHTS ON PUTTING

YOU'RE BETTER THAN YOU THINK

A few years ago, Phil Mickelson was having trouble with his putting and asked if I would spend some time on the putting green with him. I gladly invited him down to Houston. Phil is a great player and a lot of fun to be around. With Phil, you rarely start discussing the game right away; he wants to talk about airplanes, pro football, or something else for a few hours first. But when you finally get around to golf, he demonstrates a lively, creative mind. A golf conversation with Phil takes a lot of twists and turns, and he loves the give and take of a high-level debate. Sometimes he assumes a point of view just to see how well he can defend it. For instance, if Phil believes a fade is a better basic ball flight than a draw, and he senses you also prefer a fade, he might argue why a draw is better, just to see if anything constructive comes out of the discussion. He has a playful intellect that is fun and charming. It's impossible not to like him.

But on to the putting lesson that afternoon at Champions. For the first time as a pro—maybe the first time in his life—Phil's confidence with the putter had been shaken. A brilliant, instinctive putter who'd always been especially good in the clutch, Phil had experienced a series of misses under the gun that played a big part in his falling just short of winning a couple of Masters and the 1999 U.S. Open. I'd watched him falter on TV, and the root of his problem was fairly obvious to me.

When we walked onto our big putting green together, the first thing I did was find a hole on a gentle sideslope. I placed ten balls in a circle around the hole, each ball about three feet away.

"I'd like to see you make a hundred of those in a row," I said. "The rules are, you can't line up the putts, and if you miss one, you start over."

Phil gave me a look that said he didn't travel a thousand miles to perform a silly exercise like this. "I can make a hundred of those in a row easy," he replied. That was exactly what I wanted to hear.

"A hundred in a row *for how much*?" I said in my most challenging tone. I moved in a little closer, enough to make Phil slightly uncomfortable.

"How about for the best dinner in Houston?" said Phil.

"You're on," I said.

Phil missed the fourth putt. Incredulous, he immediately wanted to go double or nothing. "No thanks, I can't eat that much," I said. Standing there, just the two of us, the implications of that missed putt began to sink in to old Phil.

See, those three-foot putts weren't your basic gimmes. Each one broke a little bit differently than the last because the hole was on that mild sideslope. Each putt required a slightly different pace, fresh alignment, and a different line to the hole. Each one demanded concentration, because there was something at stake, if only a meal. To make a hundred putts in a row, even from kick-in distance, you need a consistent routine, a certain rhythm that helps you move from one putt to the next.

Far from being a gimmick, my hundred-in-a-row drill is one of the most effective I know for improving your putting under pressure. For years when I played the tour, I did this drill practically every night. Many times I would be cold, tired, and hungry, but I refused to let myself go to dinner until I made a hundred putts in succession. Early on, I discovered that after I made my eighty-ninth putt, serious pressure set in. When the hundredth putt rattled home, I felt a great sense of accomplishment. It always helped me come to the course the next day with the best attitude a golfer can have—one where you know you've paid a certain price and deserve to play well.

That drill made putting the short ones in competition almost automatic. I rarely felt that fatal twinge of doubt or fear, because I'd putted the short ones thousands of times before, including at least a hundred less than twenty-four hours earlier.

That drill rewarded me again thirty-five years after I'd retired from competition. Because at the 2004 Masters, Phil Mickelson was seen practicing the three-foot-putt drill on the practice green, and a derivation of it when he was on the course. Darned if he didn't make every pressure putt he needed on the way to winning his first green jacket.

For my "fee" that afternoon, I encouraged Phil to make a donation to our junior golf program. We all got our money's worth that day.

Why putting is difficult to teach

Putting isn't taught very well because those who teach it tend to talk about it in a linear, systematic way. There is a huge emphasis on aim and alignment, a square stance, a palms-facing grip, and setting your eyes directly over the ball. We're told to take the putter straight back and swing it straight through, keeping the face at a ninety-degree angle the whole time, and so on. I won't say any of that is incorrect—there's a good chance some of that will fit the stroke your brain tells you to make. But I don't know that it's the most effective way to teach putting.

Actually, the putting stroke is roundish in shape. It tends to follow an arc, much like the stroke in Ping-Pong. You don't want to fight that. How can the putting stroke be a straight-back and straight-through motion when you're standing sideways relative to the ball at address? To feel comfortable and execute a stroke that is easy and natural, you want the putter to travel inside the line when you take it back, the face of the putter opening a bit. Then it returns to square naturally coming through, like a door closing.

Putting is based on feel and trust. It's very difficult, if not impossible, to adopt a perfect system for putting. I believe putting is an art. It's very difficult to putt the same way every day because the creative side of you is constantly pushing for changes, adjustments, and experimentation. I've never fought that. I've used hundreds of strokes in my life, utilized a hundred variations on the same theme. At age eighty-two, I might discover a new one tomorrow. That's the fun and beauty of it. You should enjoy putting with what God gave you on a given day.

What matters most

Most of us recognize an exceptionally good putter just by seeing him make one stroke. For all the grips, stances, and strokes out

If you're a golfer who takes his putter home with him when he leaves the club, I'm betting you are one tough player to beat.

there, a great putting stroke is instantly recognizable. The person with a great stroke exudes a sense of ease. He gives the impression he's rolling the ball with his hand, which is all putting really is, except the rules say we've got to use a stick. He looks comfortable over the ball and glides into his setup just as nonchalantly, as though he were putting on a pair of shoes.

Comfort is much more important than technical perfection. Comfort isn't talked about very much because no one knows how to express it in terms relative to golf.

The old-fashioned way

The full swing has evolved some over the years, but not nearly as much as putting strokes have. If you watch films of fellows from my era, you'll notice that all of us broke our wrists very freely and used what can only be described as a "handsy" stroke. Most players today use a one-piece stroke, transporting the putter back and through with their shoulders. Their hands only come into play on longer putts, when they need to apply more speed than they can generate with their shoulders and arms alone.

Greens were so much slower in my day that we needed a fair amount of speed even on putts inside ten feet. That's one reason we let our hands into the stroke. The other reason is that it's simply a better way to putt. Regardless of the length of a putt, you'll employ better touch and timing if you allow your wrists to break going back and then "release" the putter coming through. There's a lot more touch in your fingers and the tips of your thumbs than in your shoulders, that's for sure.

I was conveying my opinion on this to a young fellow recently, and he replied rather boldly, "If your method was so good, why doesn't anybody use it?" My answer was, "They haven't got any guts." That got a laugh, and in truth, with greens as quick as they are today, I can see why players are cautious about using their hands too freely. Nevertheless, allowing a slight breaking of the wrists and releasing the head of the putter through impact is a superior way to putt, so long as you have a fine sense of touch along with confidence and trust in your ability to control the putter.

The carpenter's ninety

The style you choose is up to you. But it has to be one where the face of the putter returns to the ball at a ninety-degree angle in relation to the target. It's called "cracking a carpenter's ninety," and if you don't do it, you won't start the ball on the correct line. I don't need to mention that you'll also miss the putt.

I've always felt it was easier to control the face of the putter if I kept my hands in close to my body. I don't like my arms and hands too far from my torso. They flail away out there and the face can go anywhere.

How slow can you go?

Great putting strokes are often described as being "smooth." All that means is that there's no urgency to the motion, no sudden acceleration or jarring burst of speed. Remember, nothing good in golf happens fast. The trees and grass grow slowly, dew forms slowly, you play your best when you walk slowly. Quick is out of sync with the game.

But don't confuse a lack of urgency with lack of purpose. The

One of the most popular
putters right now has a
silhouetted image of
two balls on top of it. Now,
to putt one ball in a
straight line at the right
speed is a big job. So why
would you want a putter
with two golf balls on it,
stuck on a pole four feet
long? I mean, can
we possibly make
this game any
harder?

trick is to concentrate and be determined without letting it translate into speed.

Get close to your business

If your putting is inconsistent, you might try getting down closer to the ball. Bend more at your hips and flex your knees more. You might see the ball, the clubhead, and the line better, and you might have better control. A lot of good putters, Jack Nicklaus especially, avoided standing too tall.

Of course, if you use a long putter or a belly putter, forget that advice.

Turn the right palm down

In many ways, the putting stroke is a miniature version of the full swing. In both actions, you want to work your right palm downward through impact. Your hands have to lead the clubhead from start to finish for this to happen. Otherwise, you'll scoop the ball and won't drive it forward. Working the palm down results in solid contact and a truer roll.

As you turn the palm down, let the putter go back to the inside on the follow-through. Forcing the putter down the target line after the ball is gone has no positive effect on the stroke or your accuracy.

A putting myth

Everyone has heard how important it is to keep your head still when you putt. Certainly you want to keep your eyes riveted on the ball at address, during your takeaway, and for the better part of the forward stroke.

But not *all* of the stroke. After impact, it's fine to let your head come up and follow the ball. I think it helps your ability to roll the ball a precise distance. It's similar to the way a bowler's head comes up naturally after he releases the ball down the lane. Following through with your head and eyes is the best part of the stroke, in my opinion. People who keep their head down after impact look like they've tried to manufacture something. It's human nature to want to see where the ball went, and I see no need to fight it.

George Low

There never was a character quite like the late George Low. The son of a Scottish pro, George played the tour for a time with mixed success and is best known for being the pro that stopped Byron Nelson's streak of eleven straight victories in 1945. George didn't win that tournament; Freddie Haas, an amateur, did. But George got top money.

After he stopped playing, George followed the tour and made his living gambling, designing putters, and befriending rich people. He eventually gained the nickname "America's Guest" for the way he survived and even lived well without ever having to actually go to work.

George was a fantastic putter and something of a hustler. He putted for money with his shoe. The instep of the shoe on his right foot was customized and was flat. It was tailor-made for George to sweep his foot into the ball. He holed everything.

I bring George up because the way he putted with his shoe was something to behold. It was a totally natural motion, and anyone who went up against him quickly appreciated the importance of being relaxed and natural. It was like the man had oil in his ankles. And it helped put money in his pocket.

Every putt is a straight putt

On every putt, the ball comes off the clubface rolling exactly where the face was aimed. Somewhere along its route to the hole, there is a spot where the ball will begin to curve, or "take the break." I call that the "break point," and it's where you should aim the face of the putter as though no hole existed. The break point isn't just a matter of the line, of course. If you hit the ball firmly, the extra momentum means it will take a while to take the break.

Call it courage

Most putts, even short ones, involve some amount of break. Psychologically, it's difficult aiming to the left or right of the hole, because you're gambling that the slope of the ground will carry the ball toward the hole. It involves a certain amount of risk, and nobody likes laying odds on physics. The bottom line is that breaking putts requires courage. Many golfers have trouble summoning up enough courage to trust the break, because they're surprised that it takes courage to begin with. Give the challenge the credit it deserves, and you'll find the courage to trust the line.

On practice strokes and plumb-bobbing

Few players of my era stood by the ball and rehearsed their putting strokes. Conversely, virtually every player today makes at least a few. I wonder why. The practice strokes rarely resemble the stroke you make when you actually strike the putt. I think it's a habit ingrained when you're young, when you watched others putt. Somehow you thought it was necessary.

Putting really is in the mind, and the practice stroking I see reflects that. When I tried it, it felt awkward. I didn't know which practice stroke I wanted to put on the ball. It interrupted the clear picture I had in my mind of the line and speed. I think it's a pitiful waste of time.

The same is true with plumb-bobbing. It's just a gyration. Most players believe they're applying some sort of engineering principle when they sight the line with the shaft held in front of their faces and close one of their eyes, but it just isn't so. It's an illusion. Just ask an engineer.

The best way to sight the line is from behind the ball, from a catcher's crouch, viewing the intended path with your two naked eyes. This tells you all you need to know. Your senses are better than you think they are. After you sight the line, walk briskly to the ball, align the clubface to your target, and pull the trigger while the image is still fresh in your mind. Don't make practice strokes. You're just procrastinating.

Putting in the wind

All through the 1950s, we had bad weather at the Masters. Weather runs in ten-year cycles, and there was a long patch when there was wind, rain, and cold every year. The worst was 1956, when I made up an eight-stroke deficit on Ken Venturi. On the last day, at the par-4 seventeenth hole, I had a putt of twenty feet that was lightning quick. The greens at Augusta weren't anywhere near as fast as they are now, but that day the greens had some help. The wind was gusting to fifty miles per hour, and the sand had been blown out of the bunkers and onto the greens. There is nothing faster than a green that has a thin layer of sand on it, and if you happen to be putting downwind, forget it. I was the only player in the field whose approach shot even stayed on the seventeenth green, because it was playing downwind and was so firm and fast. Looking at this downhill putt, I almost wished my second shot had stopped short of the green. It made me sick to my stomach just looking at it.

It's funny how experience can help you. Many years earlier I had lived in Galveston, Texas, which at the time was a golf backwater. The few courses they had down there were exposed to the wind, and it wasn't uncommon for sand to blow up on them and make them slick as glass. I became accustomed to putting on them. That moment at Augusta, the memories came flooding back. I knew in my gut that a little tap would be enough to get the ball to the hole.

I also remembered the way I used to putt when the wind howled at Galveston. I made myself smaller, bending over a little more so I wouldn't be as apt to be blown off balance.

I never hit a putt more softly in my life than I did that putt on the seventeenth. At first I thought I had hit it too softly and I felt a wave of despair. I just *knew* the ball wouldn't get halfway to the hole. But then one of those fifty-mile-per-hour gusts came up and took the ball with it. The ball kept rolling and rolling and eventually dropped in the center of the cup. It was one of the luckiest breaks of my life. I was paired with Mike Souchak that day, and big "Iron Mike" pounded me on the back so hard, I had to recover for a bit before I could play the eighteenth hole.

It's asking a lot to factor in the wind when you putt. It's impossible to compose a formula that reveals how far off-line the wind can take your ball, or how much harder you have to rap the ball when you're putting into the wind. Many golfers don't allow for it at all, and some will tell you it has no effect on the ball at all. But a golf ball weighs only 1.68 ounces. Can a strong wind affect that ball as it rolls? How can it not?

The toughest read

Very often a putt appears to be straight, but you know from experience that in all likelihood it will break a couple of inches one way or the other. It's very hard to play a putt dead straight. This explains the case on TV when you see a tour pro looking at a putt from five different angles. He's trying to get a positive impression of what the ball is going to do. I think they'd get a better read (and save a lot of time) if they went at the process backward.

A putt can roll only three ways—straight, to the left, or to the right. You'll get the read much faster if you decide what the ball *won't* do. If there's a creek to the right where water tends to drain, you can eliminate the ball breaking to the left. You've already eliminated straight. So take a chance on the ball breaking a couple of inches toward the creek.

Miracles can happen

You've had days when you are unconscious, when you make every putt you look at. The next day you make nothing. Why? Because you're looking for another miracle instead of paying attention to business. Putt the same way every day. Relax, and remember that yesterday was a million years ago. You'll be surprised at how often Mr. Miracle stops in for a visit.

Never anticipate results

After all these years, the putting disease known as the "yips" remains a great mystery to players, teachers, and sport psychologists. Nobody knows for sure what causes them, and the most common cure is to use an extra-long putter. Well, if you're shaking in your Foot-Joys, you're going to be shaking in your belly and under your

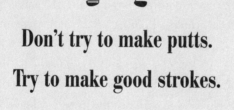

Don't try to make putts.

Try to make good strokes.

chin, too. By that, I mean it's possible to yip with the long putter, too.

I don't know of a cure for the yips, but I do know how not to get them in the first place. And that is to stop anticipating results. Many years ago, the great Kathy Whitworth missed a four-foot putt that would have meant winning a tournament. The reporters asked her what happened and she said, "I was thinking about how much I needed to make the putt instead of what I had to do to make it go in the hole." That about says it all. Assigning special importance to a putt or being aware of the consequences if you miss totally distracts you from executing the stroke. And without execution, you have nothing. Even trying to "make" putts is dangerous, because you're thinking of the objective instead of the process.

So get the cup out of your mind. Try to execute the stroke and make the ball travel on a line where the hole gets in the way. You'll never get the yips and experience the misery of shaking under your chin and in your belly.

Live with your putter

The good putter is like the good artist. He practices every day, partly to improve but mostly because it is his calling in life, a big part of who he is. Like the artist, make putting become a big part of who you are as a golfer. Like the artist, do it a little differently every time. Don't make it a science; they'll never create a robot that can make a ten-foot breaking putt on the first try. Putting is an art, the application of all your senses and imagination all at once. The great putter is admired, respected and, above all, feared.

A gift from Otey

Many putters are designed by people who don't putt well themselves. Their incompetence, fueled by the notion that the putter is to blame for their troubles, inspires them to create their own models. Such was the case in the early 1950s with Otey Crisman, a fellow who played well enough from tee to green but had nightmares on the greens. Poor putting had almost driven Otey from the tour, and his failure sparked in him a deep fascination with the subject. He began making putters in his garage in an effort to find one that would help him. It was a futile effort for Otey because the trouble wasn't the putter, it was the man swinging it. A good putter can putt with any putter at all and a poor putter can't putt with anything.

Early in 1952, I was in San Antonio hanging around with Jay Hebert, who became known for winning a PGA Championship some years later. Jay was experimenting with a mallet putter made by Otey Crisman and let me try it out. Although I liked it I gave it back to Jay, but I soon started putting so pathetically with my blade putter that I asked him to let me have another try with the mallet.

What happened next was the best run with the putter I ever had, maybe the best run by anybody, ever. I started by winning the Texas Open, shooting 64–64 in a thirty-six-hole windup. I made every putt I looked at. The next week I won the Houston Open in bad weather, again holing putts from all directions. The next stop was Baton Rouge, where more magical putting practically drove Tommy Bolt, my friend and traveling partner, insane. I was paired with Tommy during the final round, and when yet another putt would fall, I'd look at him and giggle, really rubbing it in. He was having putting troubles and he saw nothing humorous about it. I won a

A good putter can putt
with anything. Obviously
some models will feel
better to him than others.
But under duress he can
putt with a butter knife.

three-man playoff by making another long putt to beat Bill Nary—and Tommy. That made three wins in a row, and my confidence was so high I knew that all I needed to do was get the ball somewhere on the green and the Otey Crisman mallet would do the rest.

The St. Petersburg Open followed and there my putting hit its peak. It wasn't a question of whether I was going to putt well, but how well I was going to putt. I made twisting putts, long putts, all the ones in the middle, and never missed a short one. At one point I had an eight-shot lead. I won my fourth tournament in a row and to this day I'm the last player to have done that.

The only person more ecstatic than me was Otey Crisman. People all wanted to know more about my "magic" putter, and when I showed them the mallet Otey had designed, he couldn't make them fast enough in his garage. He thanked me a million times for making him comfortable financially. Of course, I thanked him, too.

Humble pie

It was the final round of the 1952 Los Angeles Open. I came to the eighteenth hole leading by one stroke, and eventually I had a putt for par that was eighteen inches long. As I got over the ball and prepared to tap in for the victory, I reflected for a moment on what I might tell the gallery during my victory speech. Lo and behold, the eighteen-incher lipped out. To make matters worse, Tommy Bolt beat me in a playoff, 71–69.

It was the biggest letdown of my career. I think about it now and wonder if I didn't hurry that putt. Maybe I didn't line it up right. For sure I got ahead of myself. Then again, maybe I just missed the putt—they don't all go in. But that's putting.

CHAPTER EIGHT

WATCHING THE DIAMONDS FALL OUT

WHY WE'RE LOSING RYDER CUPS

I've heard every reason why the American team took its worst beating ever at the 2004 Ryder Cup. We were too confident, we didn't putt very well, our teammates weren't very close to one another, the European side was more motivated to win, our styles of play weren't as flexible as the Europeans', we had five rookies, and so on. The reasons are valid. They all contributed to the 18 1/2–9 1/2 trouncing, which looked even worse up close than it did on television. I can vouch for that because I was an assistant captain.

But the most prominent reason of all came to light before the matches got under way. It just killed us at Oakland Hills and it may get us again if we don't watch out. It's an issue pervasive in all of golf and in many parts of everyday life.

It has to do with tuxedos.

On Wednesday of Ryder Cup week there was a gala dinner at the Fox Theater in Detroit. It was a big show with lots of entertainment, but to be honest I tried to get out of going. Star-studded events like that are not my cup of tea, and I also wanted to save my energy for the long days ahead. So I told M.G. Orender, the president of the PGA of America, that if it were all the same to him, I'd rather stay in the hotel and rest. M.G. was having none of it.

"We've put in a lot of expense putting this thing together, Jackie," he said. "Your tuxedo cost $3,100."

I gulped. "I guess I'm going," I said.

When I put the tux on and looked in the mirror, I looked gorgeous. My wife, Robin, looked at me and whistled. I told her, "Honey, when I die, I want to be buried in this thing. And put my old blade putter in the casket with me, because where I'm going the greens might be fast."

Those tuxedos were one of the reasons we lost. The opulence surrounding the Ryder Cup was staggering, and the tuxes were symbols of that. Players today are making millions of dollars, flying in their own jets and being treated like royalty everywhere they go. Affluence has softened them up a bit, stolen their desire to be part of a team. Add to that the major championships, a grueling schedule, and the fact that there's also another international competition—the Presidents Cup—played every two years, I think the Ryder Cup has slid a few rungs down the ladder in importance.

From the moment we landed in Detroit, we were feted with lavish gifts, world-class entertainment, and all manner of personal attention. My clothing alone probably cost $10,000. The captains, co-captains, and players each got three suits, five pairs of slacks, a jacket, four pairs of shoes (all from Oxford in England), cashmere sweaters, and a bunch of short- and long-sleeved alpaca sweaters. That was just for starters. There were six bags of stuff waiting for Robin and me in our hotel room when we got back each day. We got jewelry. They gave me a Ryder Cup ring that was so big I felt like

I'd just graduated from Notre Dame. I got a money clip encrusted with jewels I couldn't identify. We got two huge pro-style golf bags. It became almost overwhelming, and at one point I pointed at our luggage and told Robin I was concerned about how we were going to get all this stuff home.

"We'll ship it, honey," she said, patting my hand.

We had the use of sixty-six Cadillacs for the week, not that we needed them because drivers took us everywhere. The night we were driven to the Fox Theater for the gala entertainment deal, we made our entrance on a red carpet. Special chefs came in and cooked for the thousand people who attended.

Speaking of food, one room at our hotel was set aside strictly for meals and snacks. The food was the best in the world and the dessert cart was like something out of a movie. There was a night when one of the sponsors, Citigroup, sent a team of world-class chefs to our hotel. The players put on chef's hats and helped with the gourmet cooking. We ate in the kitchen with the chefs.

As you already know, the opening ceremony was like a Broadway show. I was told it was staged by the same guy who did the Super Bowl the year Janet Jackson's wardrobe malfunctioned. It all was biblical in proportion. I have to admit, I felt a little out of my element.

The players, though, didn't seem overwhelmed by the gifts. Like I said, they are too accustomed to it. You know, in the five years we conducted the Tour Championship at Champions, we received one thank-you letter. It was written by Jay Haas. I don't want to be too hard on the players on this subject; it's hard for them to say thanks when they don't know what you did to run the tournament in the first place. These are not people who have spent time

working behind a counter. They assume tournaments just pop up as an act of nature. Their job is to perform as they feel it is their destiny to do.

Before Robin and I left Houston for Oakland Hills, I got a phone call from a woman at the PGA of America. As she reviewed some of the details of what was to follow, she mentioned, "As for your transportation, we will allow you $2,000 per hour for a private plane to and from Detroit."

"Lady, I don't know who your boss is, but this has got to stop," I said. "How can you spend that kind of money?" The poor woman had no idea what to say to me.

When you inject a lot of money into a sport, a struggle ensues between art and commerce. You can focus on the art aspect—meaning the playing of the game—all you want with no ill effect. But when commerce takes over, you've had it. It happened to Greg Norman, I think. His wealth skewed his perspective on his most tragic losses by making them more acceptable. It also stole his hunger and desire.

Commerce carried the day at the Ryder Cup. The PGA of America grossed $50 million from the 2004 Ryder Cup, and it's a good thing, because it spent $40 million. The frugal side of me couldn't help but wonder if the event would have been viewed as slipshod if the PGA had spent only $30 million. I can think of a lot of programs, from junior golf to the PGA club pro, that could have used that extra $10 million. Instead, the PGA bought tuxedos for a bunch of millionaires.

Maybe the PGA of America has become intoxicated by the financial success of the Ryder Cup and can't help but try to make it bigger and bigger. Certainly the PGA has come a long way finan-

cially since my victory at the 1956 PGA Championship. My winner's check that year for $6,000 bounced because the sponsor couldn't come up with the money. The PGA, bless its heart, made good on the check. A year later at the 1957 Ryder Cup, the PGA came through with some nice bonuses for the players. We each got a free jacket, two pairs of slacks, and some shirts. That was it. For the time it was first-class treatment.

So commerce is stealing the show. To help foot the bill, tickets at the Ryder Cup cost $400 or more. There were TV interviews to do, memorabilia to sign, the wives to consider, and basically not enough time to reflect on the importance and meaning of the competition. When the matches got under way, I think we were unprepared for the pressure, the golf course, and how to handle things when we fell into a hole. Our boys tried their best, but in the end they got their butts handed to them. The commercial atmosphere wasn't conducive to playing their best golf.

And Hogan takes the checkered flag!

There came a moment when I knew our team might be in serious trouble. Our team was provided with a game room that had Ping-Pong and all sorts of video games. The players loved spending time there. One of the machines simulated car racing. As our guys took turns driving the "car," squealing with delight, something told me this was just wrong. I closed my eyes and imagined Ben Hogan sitting at the car racing game, his hat turned around backward, giggling and shouting to Arnold Palmer, who was waiting his turn.

What a nightmare. When I opened my eyes I felt like unplugging those damned machines and sending the players to their rooms.

My advice to Hal

Before the competition got under way, I wrote down a few notes to Hal Sutton. These were general thoughts I felt would be useful to convey to the team, the primary lessons that came from my own Ryder Cup experiences. Hal had so many things on his mind that he never got a chance to relate them.

1. **The higher you go, the more your ass shows—and the easier it is to kick.**

    The European team has long used the prosperity of America and its players as extra incentive to whip us good. Just as a kid from the wrong side of the tracks takes special pleasure in one-upping the rich kid from across town, so do the Europeans get a charge out of sticking it to us. It's ridiculous, of course, because their players are rich, too. Nevertheless, it gives them a reason to feel like underdogs and it binds their players together. They want to kick your ass and then watch the diamonds fall out.

    I wanted Hal to be aware of this and to make our players aware of it. Our players, deep down, feel a little guilty about being more pampered than their counterparts on the European Tour. I felt our guys could have personalized the contest a little more, because the other side sure did. It might have helped if our players had packed a little attitude. Something along the lines of "Yeah, our country has a lot. We worked and fought for it, and aren't you lucky you get to come over here and let us share it with you?"

2. The Cup never changes.

Whatever else is going on in the world, the real institutions never change. There can be wars, depressions, social troubles, or bad economies, but the Ryder Cup stands as a constant symbol of competition, sportsmanship, and camaraderie. It has tremendous value because of that, and the players should always keep that in mind. They're playing for something that is honorable, that has stood the test of time and is worthy of their respect and best efforts.

3. Jolly golf is not the way.

The players, the rookies especially, have to look past the opulence I talked about, the media attention and attendant hoopla that goes with the Ryder Cup. It is not an exhibition. It's a serious professional competition, and you'd better bring your "A" game. If you aren't prepared, your game will not hold up because this is pressure like you've never known it.

I'll never forget a moment at the 1967 Ryder Cup at Champions. Billy Casper was going off in the first match on the first day. The band from the University of Houston played the national anthem, and the American flag went up. At that moment, Billy, one of the truly great players of all time and a guy who never melted under any kind of pressure, turned to me. His face was white; he looked scared to death.

"Wh . . . wh . . . what do I do now?" Billy asked me.

"Get up there and hit that squiggly little slice of yours right down the middle," I answered.

That sort of snapped Billy to attention and he hit a fine drive.

This is not the Thursday night industrial league.

4. The least you can do is come ready to play.

I sometimes wish the captains of the individual teams were required to play. I was a playing captain in 1957 and I thought it did a lot for the team, for me, and for the media. When the captain plays, there is more speculation about the pairings, the messages from the captain to the team carry a lot of weight, and the captain is forced to be very involved. He has to play a lot leading up to the competition and thus is in closer touch with the players. It gives him more insight into his picks as captain.

I think the co-captains should be in touch, too. We definitely were out–co-captained at the 2004 Ryder Cup. One of the European co-captains, Thomas Bjorn, could easily have played on that team. He clearly was in tune with the European players. You couldn't say that about me, and Steve Jones hadn't played a lot lately, either.

5. Forget about the bonding.

I acknowledge the need for teammates to be close to one another, to share the same sense of purpose. But by the time they get to the Ryder Cup, it's too late to deal with that. The captain's hand has been dealt, and he can't waste time trying to make players like each other. If everyone gets along, great. If there's friction here and there, work around it.

There was a rumor that Phil Mickelson and Tiger Woods don't care for each other and that it was partly responsible for them getting beat twice on the first day. I don't know how true that is, but it shouldn't have mattered. They are grown men, and they should have accepted being teamed together, even relished it. Their love for their craft and the Ryder Cup should push the personal stuff into the background for four hours. They don't have to like each other, but it's a time when they definitely need to respect each other.

6. Putting is everything.

Hal Sutton is a friend whom I've visited many times over the years. One of the things I've told him is that they never give trophies away on the fairway, they are always dispensed on the putting green. In match play, putting is especially crucial because of the way it works on an opponent's mind.

With that, I wanted to remind Hal that players should spend extra time putting Oakland Hills's tough greens prior to the matches. I wanted them to really get their speed down, because the thing you want to avoid is having lots of four-footers for par. It's tough enough making them yourself when you're playing in the four-balls and singles, but when you're leaving your foursomes partner with lots of nerve-grinding short putts, sooner or later he's going to miss one—or two, or three.

7. Beat them on your own ball.

As a player, I never felt I had the mental freedom or intellect to incorporate the fine points of team play. I felt it was useful to consider beforehand who would hit first in foursomes, but once a team match started I was too focused on trying to hit the shots to worry about strategy. There's just so much stress that thinking clearly becomes difficult. You want to manage yourself as best you can, use your instincts, and just play golf.

My strategy was simple: I wanted to try to beat the other team on my own ball. I never wanted to be dependent on my partner. If he made a birdie, I considered that a bonus. I knew that if I played really well, any contribution at all from my partner would be enough to carry us to a win. I think it's a very sound approach in the better-ball format.

8. Remember the cost of losing.

You realize when the competition begins that losing the Cup would be a disaster. If you go down, you'll pay a tremendous price. You'll have let your your teammates down, not to mention having brought disappointment to an entire nation that expects you to win. You'll stand and watch the other team celebrate, and it is not a happy feeling. This is not college golf, my friend. You'll remember what happened for the rest of your life. The pressure is too great to even contemplate, so don't think about it. Tell your players to concentrate, play golf, and not think about the big picture.

Fans love "The Struggle"

When we watch the Ryder Cup, we hope in our heart of hearts that it will come down to the last hole of the last match. As spectators we crave seeing how the players will respond in this dire, desperate moment. We want it to become like the Roman arena.

Fans will pay big money to see how others will cope with what I call the Struggle. They will build a big yacht to watch a fish struggle on a line. There are people, I'm telling you, who would pay money to watch people being executed. Just to see how they handle it, you see. Ben Hogan had a hell of a struggle in life and he learned to deal with it the way he knew best, which for him was going into a shell and not talking to anybody. He was a master at handling the Struggle.

People can be bloodthirsty. When there are 30,000 people waiting for you at 2 P.M. at Augusta National on Sunday in the Masters, a lot of them are there to see if you vomit all the way down the first fairway. The player is very much aware of this. You've got a four-shot lead and they want to see if you faint sometime over the next five hours.

This is what made the 1991 Ryder Cup so compelling. When Hale Irwin and Bernhard Langer found themselves playing the eighteenth hole for the whole ball of wax, it was more than a game. It transcended into something beyond sport, into something almost primitive. The players almost lost their ability to reason. It was no wonder neither player parred the hole. It was almost too much to ask.

A dawning in the early light

When they played the national anthem at Oakland Hills, I realized once again the place sport occupies in the consciousness of our nation. Nobody in science, medicine, or even politics is idolized quite like the pro athlete. At the college level, only a tiny fraction of the student body plays football, but the athletes get more attention than any faction on campus. Let's face it, they don't play the national anthem for the English department.

One-trick ponies

A course like Oakland Hills was supposed to favor the Americans. Our guys tend to hit the ball higher than the Europeans, and that means drives won't roll into the rough and iron shots will settle quickly on those firm greens. In truth, it was tailored perfectly for the other side. It turned out the Europeans can hit the ball high, too. But when the wind came up, the Europeans came up with a lot of shots our guys either didn't have or weren't comfortable hitting. The foreigners hit the ball on low, high, and medium trajectories, and were fabulous at bouncing the ball onto the green. The Europeans were much more flexible in terms of shot selection. American players certainly can hit the ball low when they have to, but they aren't comfortable doing it.

I really came to admire the Europeans. The course conditions they see in Europe aren't uniformly perfect, and they've learned to adjust their games accordingly. At Oakland Hills, there was no type of shot they couldn't handle.

Tiger who?

I assumed the Europeans might be a little intimidated by our big guns and our home-field advantage. Man, was I wrong. I forgot that most of them have homes in America, play here most of the year, and are on a first-name basis with Tiger, Phil, and the rest. They weren't the least bit frightened. Even guys who hadn't played much in America, like Ian Poulter, were devoid of fear. They behaved like they were on vacation. They just had a blast the whole way. Our guys responded as though the pressure were all on them, even though we had the home-field advantage and were coming off a defeat in the last Ryder Cup.

The up side of terror

A lot has been made about our team being better on paper. Maybe we were, but it wasn't the best team we could have fielded. We had five rookies on the squad: Chad Campbell, Chris Riley, Fred Funk, Chris DiMarco, and Kenny Perry. Most of them hadn't played well in the months leading up to the Ryder Cup and had made the team primarily on what they'd accomplished in 2003 and early 2004. That should be changed; all points should be accumulated the year of the competition, period.

No doubt, the rookies were going to be in for a bit of a shock. I considered that when I gave Hal my proposed pairings well in advance. One of my suggestions was to pair Tiger Woods with one of the rookies. It was a time-tested idea. If you pair a rookie with a veteran, two things tend to happen. First, the veteran has little expectation of the rookie and usually plays his tail off. Second, very often the rookie is so terrified he goes into a fog and actually plays pretty well. If you can scare a point or two out of the rookies, you've got a very good chance of winning.

When a player wants to sit

Chris Riley, a nice young fellow playing in his first Ryder Cup, did a good job teaming with Tiger Woods in the Saturday morning four-balls. He then told Hal he didn't feel like playing in the four-somes in the afternoon because he was tired and had no experience playing alternate shot. It was a tough call, because it meant Jay Haas, who was close to fifty years old, would have to play again that afternoon, with virtually no rest after his morning match.

This was a tough thing to swallow. It's one thing to be hurt, but another to be "tired." My first reaction was to tell Hal to tell Chris to go out to the parking lot and wait for the rest of us, that we'd be done in about five hours. If Chris had told me he had no experience with the foursomes, I would have told him, "*Most* of us have little or no experience with them. But it works like this: He hits it, then you hit it, then he hits it again. Now get your ass out there."

But I like Chris, and his enthusiasm early on was contagious. Billy Casper, who was at Oakland Hills to take part in a corporate-sponsored exhibition before the Ryder Cup, recounted seeing Chris around lunchtime on Friday. He said Chris was pacing like a caged cat.

"I gotta get out there and root our guys on," said Riley.

"Chris, save your energy," answered Billy, an old gray fox if ever there was one. "You're going to need it."

But Riley went out on the course anyway. Like a prizefighter, he punched himself out in the early rounds.

This was not the first time I'd seen a player ask to sit on the sidelines. When I captained the team in 1973, Dave Hill came to me before the matches started and said, "I can't hit it. Don't play me." I was incredulous because it meant we had to play with essentially eleven guys instead of twelve. That's a big disadvantage when you're playing for three days.

"We can still use you," I told Dave. "You go out on the course and diagram the pin placements for us while we're inside eating our bowls of oatmeal." And Dave did that. I thought it would sort of shame him into playing, but when he said his game wasn't ready, he meant it. He only played one match the entire Ryder Cup, teaming with Arnold Palmer. I thought Arnold might carry him, but they got beat in the alternate shot by Peter Oosterhuis and Tony Jacklin.

How times have changed

The Ryder Cup to me has always been almost holy. During my heyday in the 1950s, it really was the focal point of my whole year. As a player I used it as my chief frame of reference. Week in and week out, all I tried to do was play well enough to make the team. If I accomplished that, I knew I was playing pretty darned well. I wound up playing on every U.S. Ryder Cup team in the 1950s, five altogether. I was a playing captain in 1957, and captained again in 1973.

Fifty years ago the American players had quite a different view of the Ryder Cup. We didn't know the British players very well because none of us played in Europe at all except for the British Open occasionally. Likewise, the British rarely traveled to America—there wasn't enough money on our tour to justify the trip. All we knew was they were coming over here to take the Ryder Cup away from us. And we were damned if we were going to let that happen. I think patriotism ran a little higher in those days. People didn't just stand during the national anthem, they actually put their hands over their hearts. It was a source of American pride.

Man, did we get up for it. We never thought of it as a "war" as the press and players later built it up to be. That would have been crazy, because guys like Lloyd Mangrum and Ted Kroll had been shot up in World War II and knew what real war was like. But we did view it as though something were at stake, and we weren't going to allow ourselves to lose. All of our players were close to begin with because we traveled together and stayed together. But when the American flag went up, we were brothers in arms.

The British players, I think, were attuned to that. Our nation was so much bigger than theirs and they were still recovering financially from World War II. We had more resources and better players. Maybe the biggest factor was that they didn't have the whole continent of Europe to choose from, just Great Britain. It was hard for them to look across at Sam Snead, Ben Hogan, and Cary Middlecoff and not feel distress, especially when they knew our guys meant business. We knew the Brits were a little intimidated and we took advantage of it. We beat them badly most of the time.

Take nothing for granted

The 1957 Ryder Cup was held in England at Lindrick Golf Club. It was the one team I was associated with that lost. We went down 7 1/2–4 1/2 and it hurt that I was a playing captain. The British were fantastic in the singles matches, pure magic. It was a big upset.

My lone loss as a player came during that 1957 debacle. I had a 6–0 record heading into the matches and stretched that to 7–0 when Ted Kroll and I beat Max Faulkner and Harry Weetman unmercifully in the first-day foursomes. The Ryder Cup only lasted two days back then, and there were foursomes and singles matches only, no four-balls.

At dinner after the first day, we led 3–1 and I was feeling pretty good about things. I liked our chances in the singles matches so much I had a glass of wine. There were only eight singles matches played in those days, and I wasn't going to play.

The next morning I found I *was* playing. My partner the day before, Ted Kroll, had come down with—no kidding—a chafed rear end. It happened a lot in those days, maybe because the pants we wore were so coarse. In any case, Ted's buttocks were so sore he couldn't play. I can only imagine how the media these days would handle a chafed ass.

Dai Rees, the British captain, objected to Ted withdrawing from his match. He made me go get a doctor to confirm that Ted indeed had a chafed butt and couldn't play. That hacked me off. I'd beaten Rees in the singles at Wentworth in 1953 and again at Pinehurst in 1955 with my foursomes partner, Clayton Heafner. I thought it was small of him not taking me at my word on Ted's condition. After the doctor confirmed the sorry condition of Ted's rear end, I took off my overcoat and walked to the first tee.

I felt confident filling in for Ted. My game was in good shape. Somebody asked who I was playing. "His name is Peter Mills," I said. "I've never heard of him."

"I have," somebody said. "He has a reputation for being a very shaky putter." That was music to my ears. Waiting to tee off with no warm-up, I felt pretty good about handling Peter Mills.

Well, Mr. Mills proceeded to birdie three of the first seven holes. On the other holes, he left every approach putt four feet short, and then made the tough putts for par. I couldn't get it going, and Peter Mills killed me, 5 and 3. We lost six of the eight singles matches, winning only one and tieing another. And we lost the Ryder Cup. It was the last time I felt overconfident about the Ryder Cup.

A case of putting envy

I've always been amazed at the way putting works on a player's mind. The person who can't putt deeply resents anyone who can. Ben Hogan and Sam Snead were like that. They perceived themselves as poor putters and when they got beat by someone who could putt a little, they scorned them. They were consumed by envy.

My partner in the 1951 Ryder Cup foursomes matches was Clayton Heafner. Clayton was a terrific player, a long hitter, and a fabulous shotmaker. But he wasn't a good putter, and when he played with people who could putt, he carried the type of resentment I'm talking about.

On the third hole of our match against Max Faulkner and Dai Rees, Clayton put his approach shot onto the fringe about fifteen feet from the hole. It was my turn to play, and after looking the shot over carefully, I chose to putt instead of chip. I ran the putt into the hole for a win, and looked up at Clayton for a sign of approval. That is not what he gave me. He strode toward me, frowning.

"You knew you were going to make that putt," he said accusingly. I was stunned.

"Hey man, I'm on your side," I answered. Clayton just walked to the next tee and left me standing there, shaking my head.

Settling up with Arnie

One of America's most decisive Ryder Cup victories ever was in 1967. The matches were held at Champions, Ben Hogan was our captain, and our guys poured it on from start to finish. It was pretty much over by the time the last day's singles matches got under way. But early on we knew the matches could swing either way. So when I saw that Arnold Palmer and Julius Boros were 3 down in their four-ball match to George Will and Hugh Boyle, I decided to give Arnold some extra incentive. There were nine holes left to play.

"Arnold, if you take this match to the eighteenth hole, I'll build you a wristwatch on the green," I said.

Arnold was looking for a way to get inspired, and he read into my voice a little doubt that he could get the job done.

"Just follow me," he said.

Arnold then put on the type of charge he could make in those days, and he and Boros came back and won, 1 up. Arnold saw me as he walked off the green. "So where's my watch?" he said.

Arnold needed a new watch like he needed more charisma. Over the next few days, I struggled to think of a timepiece that would rate as special. Finally it occurred to me that Arnold's first and last names together consist of exactly twelve letters. So I had a clock made up that had letters instead of numbers: A-R-N-O-L-D-P-A-L-M-E-R. I gave it to him proudly. Just last year Arnold told me he still has the clock on one of his walls in his office back home.

In praise of Ted Kroll

I've mentioned him several times already, but I want to emphasize that the best four-ball partner in history was Ted Kroll. On his own Ted was slightly better than ordinary, but as a partner I'd take him over Ben Hogan, Sam Snead, or anybody else. Ted was shot three times in World War II, and when he was your teammate, he fought like he was sharing a foxhole with you. His game was transformed. He never missed a fairway or a green and very rarely made a bogey. He never complained when you played poorly; he saw it as his mission to carry you. He was outstanding under pressure. He'd won those Purple Hearts and a four-foot putt didn't faze a guy with those experiences behind him. I won some Ryder Cup matches with Ted and a ton of money in practice rounds on tour. In fact, I don't think we ever lost.

Some players are better suited for team competition than individual play. Ted was like that. Conversely, there are some terrific players with Ryder Cup records that are surprisingly so-so. Raymond Floyd was a tough, vicious competitor in stroke play, but his Ryder Cup record was 12–16–3. Curtis Strange, twice a U.S. Open champ and a tough head-to-head player, was 6–12–2.

CHAPTER NINE

LAST CALL FOR THE LITTLE PEOPLE

WHAT GROWN-UPS SHOULD KNOW ABOUT JUNIOR GOLF

There has never been a junior golf program as large and well-intentioned as the First Tee. Since it started in 1997, the First Tee has given more than 500,000 kids their first taste of golf at more than 200 "learning facilities" across the nation. The amount of money poured into the First Tee so far has been huge. We're talking $158 million, a lot of it from corporations such as Wal-Mart and Coca-Cola. There are hundreds of volunteers running more than 160 chapters across the nation. The PGA Tour promotes it very enthusiastically. My friend George Bush, our former president, is the honorary chairman.

The mission statement of the First Tee is pretty broad. In short, the goal is to make better citizens out of the next generation by exposing them to the values associated with golf and its players. The idea is to have them learn honesty, integrity, sportsmanship, and various life skills through the game. In the end, the hope is that they'll get a leg up on being successful. Any kid can participate.

Although any kid can participate, the program seems tailored to reach youngsters who don't have the means, economically or geographically, to gravitate toward the game naturally. The motivation isn't just to help kids; golf also stands to benefit, as the First Tee is creating a well-versed generation of players for the future.

I don't dispute that golf can do an awful lot for any young person, and I also tip my hat to the volunteers who are giving of themselves to put the game within reach of as many kids as possible. But although the First Tee has its heart in the right place, I'm not convinced that any large-scale national program is the best solution to solving personal problems or bringing young people into the game.

For all the time, effort, money, and public service announcements I see during the weekend golf telecasts, I wonder if two "learning facilities" per state rate as making an appreciable difference. Will the kids have the means to keep playing golf beyond the age of eighteen, when they are no longer eligible to participate? Does it feed the malnourished kid who is too tired to walk two miles to the course? Can it fix a broken home or get a kid's parents off drugs?

What the First Tee proposes to do looks good on paper and sounds good in principle, but only time will tell how well it works out in a real-world setting. To truly learn and absorb the values expressed through golf takes long-term exposure to the game in a lot of different settings within it. They can't be taught in a series of two-hour lessons, or by handing out the rules of golf and telling kids not to talk during somebody's backswing. There is a lot of good that can be derived from golf, but it's a gradual process that requires steady exposure. The best setting isn't always a structured one. Golf only makes a strong impression when the individual immerses himself in it totally.

My feeling is that the First Tee can succeed only with supplemental support from people and clubs acting on their own. That's where the solution lies—with the public at large. Politicians and social do-gooders will say, "If we reach even one child, the $158 million was worth it." My answer to them: Let's spend a tenth of that and reach millions of kids.

My frustration with the First Tee is that it never should have been necessary. The need to build these "learning facilities" for kids stands as a black mark on the record of all local clubs and courses. What the First Tee and its volunteers have spent $158 million and untold energy trying to do could be done at the local level on a more cost-effective basis and could reach millions of kids instead of a few hundred thousand. It goes back to the same old problem: club members trying to get a lot out of the game without wanting to give anything back. Most clubs aren't particularly concerned about where the game might be a generation from now, and clang the gates of the club closed behind them.

There are about 17,000 clubs in America. I believe each one of them should conduct outings for kids (and I don't mean children of the members) three times a year. You conduct a clinic, let them play a few holes, give them some lunch, and talk to them. You invite them out to caddie, which is a great way for a kid to start out, as they get to play the course for free on Mondays. Now, if every club did that, and you had the First Tee running besides, you'd really have something. This is what we do at Champions, and though it's no panacea, I do know that if every club in Houston did the same, we'd have some fertile ground a lot of golfers could grow from.

"C'mon, little Jack"

No doubt about it, kids these days are in crisis. Drugs and gangs are everywhere, proper education and sound guidance from parents are lacking, and the world situation we've left them with is as complicated as it's ever been. Not having a place to play golf is the least of their problems. That's why I applaud the First Tee for addressing the challenges kids face in general, even if golf has a limited capacity to solve them.

In a perfect world, every young golfer would be brought up the way I was. I was very lucky to be raised in a "good house." A great many kids come up in bad houses—a broken home, abusive circumstances, or tough financial conditions. Throughout my life, I've tried to take a person's background into account when I measure them. A certain percentage of what they are is due to the luck of the draw.

In our house, work, discipline, self-reliance, and honesty were pervasive. But it wasn't like being raised in a monastery. Golf was all around us, of course, and I started playing at age six. My first memory is of trotting after a woman who let me accompany her during her rounds at River Oaks Country Club in Houston. I hazily remember watching her and her letting me take a swing from time to time. Her given name was Quo Vadis Quayle, but by the time we met her last name was Burke. She was my mother.

I was a fairly small, frail kid, and by the time I was nine I had developed asthma something terrible. Any exertion at all would get me gasping for air, and I couldn't play other sports. Dad felt I had to get exercise somehow, and he'd have me sit and watch him give lessons to the members. He was a strong believer that the golf swing is essentially a throwing motion, and he literally would have his pupils throw clubs out on the range. He would tell them to release the club just after impact, and if the club whirled where the pupil was aiming, he was releasing the club correctly. My job was to retrieve the clubs. I'd run out and collect the clubs and return them to the teaching station, by which time I'd be out of air. I'd recover just in time to run out and collect the clubs again. I've never forgotten Dad's throwing principle, incidentally; I still believe the golf swing is a throwing action.

So I absorbed a lot about golf just watching my dad. I also learned how to address adults, how to behave at the table, and how to dress neatly. By the time I reached my early teens, I was an avid player and well-behaved enough that my parents felt comfortable putting me on my own in front of some of our famous guests. One of them was Babe Didrikson Zaharias, who started concentrating on golf in the mid-1930s. She played at River Oaks all the time and sometimes needed somebody to play with. She'd come into the shop looking to go play, and she'd look at me and say, "C'mon little Jack, let's tee it up," and my heart would beat out of my chest. She turned out to be an ideal playing companion for me. She was a fierce competitor and serious about the game, but she also was a lot of fun to be around.

Babe wasn't so good at that early stage of her career that I couldn't give her a game. What I couldn't do was outdrive her. Babe sensed, correctly, that distance is a great weapon in golf. Raw as her game was, she really belted the ball. Her philosophy was that she'd utilize her strength and speed from the outset and acquire control later. I was smaller than she was and tried my best to drive my ball past hers. I went after the ball pretty aggressively, too, my competitive desire to keep up with her overtaking any attempt to hit the ball straight. I was lucky to go up against her, because that is the way you teach a kid to play golf—swing the club as fast as you comfortably can from the get-go, with plenty of recklessness, and learn to find it later on. You can teach control, but power is a hard thing to add to a golfer's repertoire.

One day Babe caught a drive just flush. When it was my turn to play, I also hit it right on the screws. When we got to our balls, my drive was past hers. Babe came over and squeezed my biceps, acknowledging that my drive was no fluke. I was red with pride. The day I outdrove Babe was one of the greatest days of my life.

The need for spontaneous play

It's human nature to perceive the past as being better than it actually was, which is one reason the thought of sitting in a rocking chair scares me so much. But I do feel it's tragic that children today are denied something my generation enjoyed as a birthright. I'm talking about every child's right to play. I mean spontaneous, reckless, unsupervised, prolonged play with other children. We've observed that children are overweight, unhealthy, addicted to video games and overly influenced by television, yet somehow see the solution—play—as being fruitless and wasteful.

When we were children, there were times of the year when we played outdoors all day long. We played hard, sweaty games that went on for hours, many of which we made up on the spot, played once and never played again. Left to our own devices, we worked our bodies and imaginations. We learned to compete, negotiate, argue, and improvise. I don't need to tell you that not many of us were overweight, bored, sick, or in need of Ritalin. The results of that are hard to measure, but I think it made us better, healthier adults.

Play today is seen as frivolous. We're terrified of our kids falling behind intellectually and feel the way to prepare them for adulthood is to shorten summer vacation and start teaching algebra in sixth grade. We adults are also scared for them—we don't even want them walking to school, which is good exercise, for fear of them getting hit by a car or kidnapped. Those are valid concerns. But we've got to find a way to put play back into their lives. We've about given up on that idea.

The city of Houston has never built a golf course. If you go down to get one approved, some politician will object, "Shouldn't we be building schools?" and that's the end of it. I say, schools hardly let kids out for recess anymore. They have nowhere to go after school, no arenas where they can play. If more places existed—the golf course is only one of many venues that would work—they'd have something to do after school and would be better able to avoid trouble. I don't know that jobs are the answer. How often can a kid sweep out the garage? Let them be kids.

As I see it, if a city develops 200 acres and doesn't devote 10 percent of it to a park or recreation area, the politicians behind it should have hell to pay. It's just so obvious that play is constructive and not a waste of time. And golf is perfect for that.

Starting a kid in golf

Many parents are unsure when they should get their children started in golf. These days the question is usually answered for them. A lot of courses are duly concerned about liability and have a minimum age requirement, which is unfortunate. But you should try to take them somewhere where such a policy isn't in place and as quickly as possible after the kid asks if he can go. If you're a golfer and a fan who watches the game on TV, that will be around age six or seven. But don't rush it if it takes longer.

The best approach is to let the child walk along with his parent.

Let him swing once in a while, any way he wants. Throw a ball out once in a while and let him give it a whack, then make him pick it up. It should be no more than exercise and companionship. The reason he chose to go is that you're taking an interest in him. Spending time with him is a huge gift.

There should be no instruction. That's a tall order, but you have to discipline yourself to avoid it. If you start telling him where his Vs should point, a six-year-old might end up crying with frustration. Instead, tell him what the lake, bunker, and flagstick are for.

If there's a junior program, don't start him out there. Even rudimentary programs are a little too structured and too much for a child to handle. He'll get there soon enough. Your first job is to get him used to hitting a ball with stick at such a level that he doesn't whiff every other swing.

Using the practice area
Surely some of your time with your child will be spent around the practice area. The best way to use it is to start your child near the hole—and I mean close up. Let him get used to holing three-foot putts. It will help teach him what the basic stroke is about, and the success he experiences will encourage him to keep trying.

Gradually move farther away. Chipping comes next, then sand shots, then the full shots. This is a great way to teach and learn. You know who learned the game this way? Tiger Woods.

Incidentally, this is a great way for the adult beginner to learn, too.

Monkey see, monkey do
Kids learn by observing. The main reason there are more excellent junior golfers than ever before is the huge number of excellent mod-

els they get to watch on TV. Young people are eager to imitate their heroes and are very adept at it. I can't overstate the advantage kids have by getting to see Ernie Els or Annika Sorenstam virtually every night on the Golf Channel. It's not just the number of good swings, it's the lack of poor ones. There are very few unorthodox, unusual swings at the pro level. You have to go all the way to the Champions Tour to find some really distinctive swings, and they exist only because there wasn't much TV when guys sixty and older were coming up.

Texas has always produced an inordinate number of great players, more so than practically any state other than California. The weather—lots of wind and rain, extremes of heat and cold—has a lot to do with that, as does strong competition. The state's heritage of fine players has been important, too. Ben Hogan, Byron Nelson, Tom Kite, Ben Crenshaw, and many others didn't have a lot of television growing up, but they sure had a lot of good swings to look at when they were young. The game got a late start down here, but it took root very strongly. Anybody who grows up playing golf in Texas has a built-in advantage over players who enjoyed nicer weather, but insufficient standards of good play and strong competition.

Nowadays, though, good players can come from anywhere. And it's the ability to imitate the players on television and at the club that is helping a lot of kids break 75 on tough courses by the time they get to high school. What they learn by watching makes a more emphatic impression than what you can explain verbally, or show them on a computer. Rhythm and timing can't be explained, only absorbed by osmosis. That's the value of golf on television.

Children have to play a lot, and they need a lot of freedom to develop ideas on their own. Watching a kid adopt the mannerisms and swing of his favorite pro, and then inject a little bit of his or her own style, is a joy. Inevitably they will experiment, and a lot of things they try won't work. They'll get frustrated from time to time, and even that's tolerable to watch because it shows they care.

Sissies no more

It's almost hard to believe, but only twenty years ago golf was still considered a sissy game in some circles. As most people saw it, if you played golf, you might be a sissy, and if you played tennis, you were a sissy for sure. Golf was the repository of the small and weak, the game chosen by kids who couldn't excel at baseball or football. All the best players were short, if not weak. Bobby Jones, Ben Hogan, Arnold Palmer, Jack Nicklaus, and the vast majority of great players of the twentieth century were less than six feet tall. There were a few notable exceptions, such as Byron Nelson and Dr. Cary Middlecoff, but conventional wisdom held that height and size were detriments. Golf was also the only sport in which infirm individuals had a chance to excel. Ed Furgol had a badly withered right arm and won the U.S. Open. Casey Martin, beset by a bad leg that necessitated the use of a cart, couldn't have played professionally in any other sport but golf.

It's incredible how these notions came undone over a period of just a few years. Today, the top four players in the world are six feet tall or taller. Tiger Woods, Ernie Els, Phil Mickelson, and Vijay Singh are not only tall, they are strong and exceptionally athletic. The trend is here to stay, especially at the pro level. The real up side to golf becoming a "sport" as much as a "game" is that it's more acceptable for kids to wear their love of golf on their sleeves and hail these guys as heroes. There was a time when I never thought I'd see a golfer making a Nike commercial.

Despite the best players getting bigger, golf will always be a game in which a short, small-boned person can excel, especially at the amateur level. Golf is tremendously appealing to kids because they quickly find that good timing and technique can make the ball go pretty far. And it should be the game of choice for parents, because of all it does for a young person physically, emotionally, and socially.

Out latest prodigy, Michelle Wie

There may not be any studies to back me up, but I've noticed that kids who grow large physically at an early age tend to develop faster emotionally as well. Child prodigies such as Michelle Wie need every bit of that maturity. It's hard to imagine what the world looked like through her thirteen-year-old eyes when she almost made the cut at the men's Sony Open in Hawaii a couple of years ago, or when she teed off with the 54-hole lead in the 2005 U.S. Women's Open. If you'd put me in her spot at that age, I'm sure I would have been terrified. But her maturity level matches every inch of her six-foot height. She handles all the pressure with a lot of poise. There's no question that, for the rest of her life, she'll be older emotionally than others her age.

Whether early success is healthy or not is a moot question, because that train has already left the station. She hasn't lived a "normal" life from the time she was watching cartoons, and there's no way the remainder of her teen years will bear any resemblance to what passes for ordinary. She'll pretty much miss her teen years completely. By the time she turned pro in 2005 at age fifteen, emotionally she was closer to twenty. It's a case of someone always occupying an unusual station in life.

I don't go along with those who see extremes of good or bad in the way she's been brought along. It's too early; we have to see how the story plays out. It's all a question of whether she can not just survive, but prosper. In the coming years she's going to get a lot of good advice from people who are familiar with the challenges she'll face. She'll also get some bad advice. It all depends on the ability of her parents, her manager, and Michelle herself to distinguish the good advice from the bad. It's a harrowing game. She has more at stake than most people.

As for her game, she obviously knows how to hit a golf ball. But learning to hit the shots is the easy part. I'm more intrigued by how well she will utilize her skills commercially now that she's turned pro. Make no mistake, her turning pro and becoming a star is what this is all about. Cashing in commercially is the end game for a pro; it's the bottom line.

It's very important that her parents have a grasp now of what's going to happen, and to help make the right decisions for her—and them. They have a lot at stake, too, because they'll be asked to answer for her success or failure. I'm pulling for all of them. They mean well and she's a good kid.

Fun and games, plus a firm hand

Youngsters need to know that golf is a privilege, not a right. Golf can teach discipline, decorum, respect, and good manners, but only if kids are guided by a friendly but firm hand.

At this writing, we have roughly forty juniors at Champions.

They are allowed to play practically any time, carrying their own bags. They play the front nine in about an hour and a half, buy a drink at the refreshment stand, then sail around the back nine. It's a big deal to them, but there are rules. The players are each given a player's card before they tee off. Throughout the round they are observed to see if they're caring for the course properly—raking bunkers, fixing ball marks, replacing divots, and so on. Caring for the course isn't a suggestion, it's a rule. If a kid gets out of line with these tenets, his card is confiscated by the course marshal and he can't play for thirty days. He has to go back to his parents and tell them what happened. Eventually he is given the card back.

It sounds harsh, but in fact, the kids never get in trouble. The kids would rather lose one of their legs than forfeit that card. They don't like being confronted by their parents, and the thought of being shamed and embarrassed in front of their friends is a powerful deterrent. Kids need rules. They actually *like* them. Putting a few in place is a great way to keep the peace and groom our young people into being good golf citizens.

CHAPTER TEN

BETWEEN ROUNDS

HOW TO GO 1-UP ON LIFE

There is roundness everywhere in golf.

The ball, the cup, the greens, the flagstick, and the dime you mark your ball with are round. The canopies formed by the trees, the puffy cumulus clouds in the sky, and the planet we play on are rounded. The shapes we make, from the rotation of our bodies to the orbs we trace with our golf clubs, are circular. We golfers are round all over, from our eyes down to our kneecaps. The game, its environment, and its players are a study in circles, spheres, curves, and arcs.

One reason we love golf is that it puts us close to nature. In nature, straight lines and sharp angles are an aberration. I've come to believe there is a metaphysical side to golf, and that to play the game well and obtain maximum satisfaction and enjoyment from it, we must approach it in a relaxed, creative, "round" way. The game rewards those who keep in step with its rhythms and harmonies. That's why I've always preferred teaching through feel, demonstration, mental images, and simple explanations. That's the artistic way, one that is in keeping with the elemental nature of the game.

Life's challenges should be approached in a similar way. Most problems are more easily overcome by creativity and patience than by sheer force of will. Admittedly that's hard to do in an age where things move so fast and we're pushed to be expedient.

Life today tempts us to overcome difficulties as quickly as possible. There is less time to reflect on challenges and come up with creative ways of solving them. So we tackle them head-on. Money problems at home? Put in more hours. The coach doesn't produce a winning record within two years? Fire him. The third-grade class comes up short on testing scores? Give them homework and lengthen the school year. There is a decided lack of imagination being put toward problem solving these days.

When fellows my age refer to the "good old days," we're pining for an era when leisure time was more readily available, the pace of living was slower, and we lived in a world devoid of cell phones, computers, and cable TV. I don't know that life was any easier, but it certainly was less complicated and less stressful.

I hope you find some of the following tips useful. They constitute part of my approach to life in general.

Father Allnoch's confession

I grew up attending an all-boys Catholic school. The priests who taught us were no-nonsense types who were big on discipline. More than one of us had a red backside to prove it.

The math class was taught by one Father Allnoch, a man I'll never forget. He meant business all the time. One day Father Allnoch walked into the classroom and the students, as usual, stopped talking at once. He said, "I can tell this class isn't going to go very far in the world, but if you pay attention to what I'm going to tell you right now, you just might make it."

He walked to the front of the classroom and drew a line down the center of the blackboard. He then wrote in chalk on one side of the blackboard a large "51." Then he took a few steps sideways and wrote "50" on the other side.

"If you make this," he said, tapping the number 50 with the piece of chalk, "don't spend this"—and he moved sideways and tapped the number 51.

That's the best lesson in economics I ever received. In a day when so many things are bought on credit, I flat-out refuse to go into debt except when absolutely necessary.

One result of my fiscal policy is that I'm sometimes accused of being tight with a dollar. Another result is that in the forty-nine-year history of Champions Golf Club, we've never levied an assessment on our members. Not many clubs can say that. If more people—including our elected officials—put that philosophy into effect, we'd all be better off.

Your long-range goal
Live your life so that when you die, you fill up the church. A big funeral says something about how much you were loved, or at least respected. These people who get to the church by way of the electric chair don't generate much of a turnout. They have to rent the pallbearers.

Never quit working
When you are around clubs all your life, you encounter people who retire from business at a relatively young age and fulfill their dream of playing golf every day. But early retirement isn't what it's cracked up to be. The retired businessmen tend to huddle with

each other, because that's what they did when they were in business. You overhear them talking about the price of screwdrivers at Home Depot. They get sick of golf; you never see them smiling when they're coming up eighteen. They are bored silly.

The early retiree ends up pining for the aggravation he experienced when he worked for a living. He realizes that the reason the golf course seemed like heaven was because it provided relief from the hassles he went through at work every day. If you remove the aggravation, you also remove the feeling that you are being rewarded for your effort at your job.

I still go to work every day, though sometimes for only half a day. I believe I was put on this earth to produce. I suppose I could putter around the garden all day or get caught up in the plot of some daytime soap opera, but the thought of that truly frightens me. I'd know I was one step closer to the cemetery.

Leaving the stage

Despite my feelings about retirement, there does come a time in life when you need to shift gears and move away from your primary source of accomplishment. When age robs you of your ability to perform as well as you did in your heyday, it's time to do something else. That's very hard to do, especially for high-profile people. They fight to hang on. Movie stars get facelifts, network news anchors go down kicking and screaming, and athletes continue to perform for so long that the public forgets how good they were in their prime.

At a Masters dinner not far back, I brought with me a small section of rope. When I said hello to Arnold Palmer, I held the rope out and said, "Arnold, this is for you."

"What's that?" Arnold asked.

"It's a gallery rope, Arnold, and it's time for you to join the rest of us on the other side of it." That practical joke contained a real point, which I'm sure Arnold understood.

I care about Arnold and am thankful for the massive contributions he's made to our game. I realize that many people still love seeing him perform, but watching him struggle on the golf course hurts. At least one generation has no idea what a magnificent player he was. It's similar to watching Muhammad Ali and Willie Mays toward the ends of their careers.

Arnold is lucky. When other athletes descend from the tops of the trees, they break a lot of branches on the way down. He's coming down with angel wings.

Consider being considerate

I get a lot of handwritten notes. The trouble is, I can't read anybody's writing. The average person's handwriting is no better than a doctor's. Hell, I'll present the note to the person who wrote it, and half the time *they* can't read what they wrote. I think we're in a national crisis that way. Everything you do, from writing the letter "B" to making a routine phone call, should be done with others in mind. The considerate person is eventually repaid tenfold.

By executive order

President Dwight D. Eisenhower once said that the good farmer tries to leave the land in better shape than he found it. This is why we should replace our divots and repair our ball marks. It also is why we should pick up somebody else's litter or move a grocery carriage out of an empty parking spot without expecting to get a medal for it.

Career advice

If you're working for a company that is obsessed with numbers, sales projections, and the bottom line, quit tomorrow. Go to work for an outfit that cares what Tiger Woods cares about: execution. It's easy for some hard-ass boss to give his guys numbers they have to meet, then kick back and just expect it to happen. He gives you a problem but no solution except "work harder." If you ask him how to do it and his eyes move away, it's time to leave.

On playing the market

I was telling a friend how many stock tips I get and how confusing it all is. He said, "Every time I get a tip, I act on it. I buy another hundred shares of AT&T."

Lower your risk

If you're thinking of investing money in a company, study it and make sure it satisfies three criteria: (1) They're hiring people, not firing them; (2) they're paying their bills on time; and (3) their inventory isn't too big (a sign there's a demand for their product and they're adept at moving it). If a company is doing those three things, it's doubtful you'll get hurt.

A sure-fire winner

In all my life, I've never seen a mirror shop go out of business. Everyone is drawn to mirrors. Most people can't help but look at their reflections when they pass a storefront window. It comes down to this: Young people want to see how pretty they are, and old people are looking to see how old they are.

A brand-new you

Life is about reinventing yourself. You have to reinvent the wheel every day. It's all about doing things differently, putting a new presentation on your approach to people, and solving problems. If you have the mental flexibility to do that, you're way ahead of the game, whether it's golf or anything else.

Humble pie

One day a fellow presented himself to me as being a "self-made man." I said, "You must be the first SOB who ever came out of the womb self-made." We all learn from other people. We need other people. I've had 30,000 teachers in my lifetime. We all have.

Al Balding's discovery

One of my better friends on tour was Al Balding. A Canadian, Al was a good player and always good company. One night at dinner he showed me a squib he'd written on a scrap of paper. It read, "I think I've stopped looking for the trouble before it happened, worrying about mistakes before I make them."

A lot of lessons are wrapped into that. It says you want to be decisive, not tentative, in your decision making. It speaks of the importance of positive thinking. It talks about living in the present, not the past or the future. Most of all, it cautions against anticipating results.

One tough boss

After I returned home from my stint in the Marines during World War II, I was at a loss for how I would resume my life. I played in a few tournaments, but wasn't making much money and really needed a full-time job. To my rescue came Craig Wood, a fine champion who, in addition to winning a couple of majors, also had the distinction of losing all four major championships in playoffs. Craig was the pro at Winged Foot and was an old friend of the family. He was very well connected, and he put in some calls and got me an assistant pro job at the Hollywood Club in Deal, New Jersey.

The head pro at the Hollywood Club was a Scot by the name of George Fotheringham. Although I'd spent a few years in the Marines, I never knew what a tough job was until I went to work for this man. He was almost impossible to deal with, an unbelievably demanding man whose approach to work was almost biblical. He also was the most tight-fisted person ever put on this earth. He refused to pay me until the members paid *him*, and that took some time. Once, a few of his practice balls got mixed in with mine, and when he found out, he deducted the cost of the well-worn balls from my pay.

After a year at Hollywood, I got a better job at Winged Foot. When I told Craig Wood about the misery Mr. Fotheringham put me through, Craig laughed. "I knew if you could put in a year under that Scotsman without quitting or getting fired, you'd be a success in life," he said.

I think all young people should have the experience of working for a tough boss. It will shape their character, instill a sound work ethic, and make them realize that no one should expect to go through life without paying some dues.

Smoking and drinking

As a young man I didn't just smoke cigarettes, I practically ate them. My on-course policy was to light one up when I made a bogey or a birdie. Then came a tournament in Philadelphia. I was five under par early in the round and on the next hole had a fifteen-footer for birdie. I wanted a cigarette and asked my caddie for some matches. I'd told him never to come out without a book of matches, but this time he didn't have any. The putt was an easy one, but when I got over the ball I got to thinking, "This sure would be easier if I had a cigarette." I was distracted and missed the putt.

Walking across a bridge on the way to the next tee, I finally got my cigarette lit. I told my caddie, "This is the last cigarette I'm ever going to even look at. I quit." That was in 1962. And I haven't had one since. Like everyone else who has quit, I'm glad I gave them up—which isn't to say I didn't enjoy them.

Smoking, drinking, and golf have always walked hand in hand. At Champions we banned smoking indoors ten years ago, largely because of health reasons—if a worker gets sick, he'll miss a day or two of work, which is bad, and he might sue you, which is worse. Plus, they smell up the building. The smokers complained at first, but eventually they got used to it. In twenty years, smoking may very well cease to exist.

As for drinking, most clubs realize that DWIs are serious and they don't want to be held responsible for them. People are going to drink, and it's wise for the club to have a sober employee or two around to give them a ride home.

On drugs

It's not enough to tell children not to use drugs. I don't think the "just say no" message is sufficient. Parents should make it clear that people who use drugs are yellow cowards who hide behind whatever substance they're on. Kids must know that the real tough guy faces his life, pays his taxes, raises his kids, and buys the goods that help keep people employed. Tell them that living an upstanding life takes courage, and praise them when they do right.

Three cheers for the family man

I'm sometimes asked who is the greater golfer, Jack or Tiger? My answer is Nicklaus, by a wide margin. I believe Jack is one of the most extraordinary athletes of all time. He compiled a playing record that is the standard by which all other golfers are compared, Tiger especially. Moreover, Jack did it while raising five children—and raising them well. Jack is blessed with a wonderful wife who looked after the children every day. But Jack always had an active role.

Tiger has a ring on his finger now, and it may not be long before he changes his first diaper. When that day comes, we can really start to talk.

My favorite quotes

The mere athlete becomes too much of a savage, and the mere musician is melted and softened beyond what is good for him. The two should therefore be blended in right proportions.

—PLATO

It's hard to get lost on a straight road.　　　—ANONYMOUS

It is doubtful if a great man ever accomplished his life's work without having reached a play interest in it.

—JOSEPH LEE

Leisure is the mother of philosophy.   —THOMAS HOBBES

Play is defined not by the type of activity engaged in but by the distinctive attitude which the players take toward the activity. In play, it is the activity itself rather than the results which count.   —ENCYCLOPEDIA OF MODERN EDUCATION

When I go down, don't lower the flags. Leave them up. I am on the way to find the head pro and get a starting time.

Jack Burke Jr.

A C K N O W L E D G M E N T S

I extend my warmest thanks to three good men:

Nick Seitz for his deft editing of the raw manuscript.

Bud Shrake for some great advice before we began writing.

Jim McLean for caring so much the whole way.